BRITAIN'S BEST POLITICAL CARTOONS 2021

Dr Tim Benson is Britain's leading authority on political cartoons. He runs the Political Cartoon Gallery and Café which is located near the River Thames in Putney. He has produced numerous books on the history of cartoons, including *David Low Censored*, *Giles's War*, *Churchill in Caricature*, *Low and the Dictators*, *The Cartoon Century: Modern Britain through the Eyes of its Cartoonists*, *Drawing the Curtain: The Cold War in Cartoons*, *Over the Top: A Cartoon History of Australia at War* and *How to be British: A Cartoon Celebration*.

D0474669

BRITAIN'S BEST POLITICAL CARTOONS 2021

Edited by Tim Benson

HUTCHINSON
HEINEMANN

For Bobbie and Desiree Benson

1 3 5 7 9 10 8 6 4 2

Hutchinson Heinemann
20 Vauxhall Bridge Road
London SW1V 2SA

Hutchinson Heinemann is part of the
Penguin Random House group of companies whose addresses
can be found at global.penguinrandomhouse.com.

Penguin
Random House
UK

First published in the United Kingdom by Hutchinson Heinemann in 2021.

www.penguin.co.uk

A CIP catalogue record for this book is available from the British Library.

ISBN 9781786333131

Typeset in 11/15.5 pt Amasis MT Light by Jouve (UK), Milton Keynes

Printed and bound in Italy by L.E.G.O. S.p.A.

The authorised representative in the EEA is Penguin Random House
Ireland, Morrison Chambers, 32 Nassau Street, Dublin D02 YH68

Penguin Random House is committed to a sustainable future
for our business, our readers and our planet. This book is made from
Forest Stewardship Council® certified paper.

MIX
Paper from
responsible sources
FSC® C018179
FSC
www.fsc.org

INTRODUCTION

Should **pocket cartoons** ever be considered in the same category as political ones? I raise this question mainly because a number of pocket cartoonists believe they have been unjustly pigeon-holed by people like myself who treat their work as substantially different from that of political cartoon-ists. They have complained that, although their work regularly appears in the same newspapers that feature political cartoons, they do not receive the same attention as their larger-scale counterparts. Indeed, large-scale, finely drawn political cartoons have long been celebrated and many have become iconic, from James Gillray's 'The Plumb-pudding in Danger', to John Tenniel's 'Dropping the Pilot', to David Low's 'Rendezvous'. Pocket cartoons – small-format, economically drawn, topical gags – are certainly popular, but, as James Whitworth, a pocket cartoonist whose work features in the *Sheffield Telegraph*, *Private Eye* and others, wistfully points out, they have, overall, received less attention from cartoon enthusiasts. It has even led to some pocket cartoonists complaining about their exclusion from this anthology over the last few years. So, are there fundamental differences in the form and function of pocket and political cartoons? And is my exclusive focus on political cartoons justified?

Of course, one must bear in mind that political cartoons have the advantage of having been around for over 300 years. The first pocket did not appear in the British press until just 82 years ago – 3 January 1939, to be precise – and it came about purely by chance. The poet John Betjeman had been commissioned to write a series on archaeology for the *Daily Express* and had asked Osbert Lancaster, at that time an architectural historian and illustrator for the *Architectural Review*, to assist him. One night over dinner, Lancaster happened to mention to the *Express*'s features editor, John Rayner, how much he admired the little column-width cartoons that regularly appeared in the French newspapers and wondered why they had never caught on in the British press. To Lancaster's rather pleasant surprise (given that the *Daily Express* had at that time the largest circulation in the world for a national newspaper), Rayner replied, 'Go ahead, give us some.' Lancaster did so and Rayner duly labelled them 'pocket cartoons' in reference to the German 'pocket battleships' that were then constantly in the news.

Lancaster's first cartoons were positioned in Tom Driberg's 'William Hickey' gossip column. Driberg, who had known Lancaster from his days up at Oxford, was more than happy with them. 'They had the additional merit,' Driberg joked, 'of relieving me of about three inches of writing space.' Lancaster's cartoons were immediately distinctive. Whereas contemporary political cartoonists such as David Low were busy skewering the likes of Hitler and Mussolini, Lancaster's cartoons were more generally observational, finding the humour in everyday life. He particularly enjoyed poking gentle fun at the English upper classes, their fashions, political views, and responses to social change. Over time, he developed a cast of characters, not least Maudie, Countess of Littlehampton, whom he used to satirise the establishment to which he belonged.

Such was the popularity of Lancaster's cartoons that, when war did break out, they were transferred to the front page. This was something of an enigma to the newspaper's proprietor, Lord Beaverbrook, who once asked his aide, George Malcolm Thomas,

"No, I asked them to leave me out this year. There comes a time when any additional honour is merely an added burden."

Osbert Lancaster's first cartoon for the *Daily Express*. Published on 3 January 1939, the cartoons ridicules the much-decorated grandees who were recipients of the 1939 New Year's Honours, as well as those that missed out.

Osbert Lancaster at work on his daily cartoon in June 1944.

'What is the point of Osbert Lancaster?' (The hostility was mutual: 'He was a bastard,' Lancaster said of the proprietor.) In spite of Lord Beaverbrook's puzzlement, Lancaster's cartoons remained on the front page. In fact, as Lancaster later recalled, the war gave him an unexpected advantage: 'Then there was a stroke of luck, the war started and there was paper rationing. All the other cartoonists were given less space, and I remained the same size. It made me look much more important.'

As wartime restrictions drove 24-page broadsheets down to four large pages and 36-page tabloids down to eight small pages, the benefits of pocket cartoons became apparent to other news papers, too. Within a matter of months, Roland 'Neb' Niebour's pocket cartoons began appearing in the *Daily Mail* and Frederick Joss's in the *Star*. 'It is easy to understand the editorial popularity of the pocket cartoonist, in these days of paper shortages,' a 1942 piece in the *London Opinion* said. 'The artist who can get his joke across in a couple of square inches of newsprint is a man after the editor's own heart.' Even Hitler seems to have been a fan. When the ruins of his chancellery in Berlin were pored over in May 1945, a cutting of one of Neb's pocket cartoons, from the *Daily Mail* of 15 January 1945, was found among the ruins.

The post-war years saw the arrival of the first female pocket cartoonists, among them Margaret Belsky. Belsky, who began working for the *Daily Herald* in 1951, regarded herself modestly as 'just a hack' and 'the poor man's Osbert Lancaster', although she drew over 6,000 cartoons for the paper and was the first woman to draw a front-page cartoon for a national publication. Antonia Yeoman,

"Of course I've saved them—they're bound by law to give me my job back, after the war."

—by Neb.

The Roland 'Neb' Niebour cartoon that was found among the ruins of Hitler's chancellery. By January 1945, Germany had exhausted its resources on the Western Front and Soviet forces were closing in from the east, so Hitler may well have been nostalgic about his years earning a living as a painter in Vienna. The day after the cartoon was published, Hitler took up residence in the *Führerbunker*, where he stayed until his death.

who worked for *Punch* in the 1950s, was also widely admired and similarly understated about her talents. She once told an interviewer, 'I wake up in the morning in terror wondering if I'll be able to think of any more jokes . . . I'm not really interested in politics or news, so that makes it difficult.' However, the prejudice against female cartoonists at the time meant that both felt obliged to hide their gender. Margaret Belsky used only her surname, while Antonia Yeoman signed her cartoons 'Anton'.

By the time Osbert Lancaster retired in 1981, he had produced in excess of 10,000 cartoons. Drawn on any old scrap of paper that came to hand, rarely signed, and crudely and speedily drawn, his later cartoons do not represent his finest work as an artist. But Lancaster's popularity was such that his work had spawned a new breed of pocket cartoonists in both broadsheet and tabloid newspapers. Several of the most prominent took Lancaster's minimalism a step further. Rudimentary figures with simple bulbous noses were the hallmark of Mel Calman and Bryan McAllister's work in the 1970s. David Austin in the *Guardian*, Mark Boxer (who used the pen-name 'Marc') in the *Observer*, Tony Holland at the *Daily Telegraph* and Barry Fantoni in *The Times* followed a similarly stylised, if individually distinctive, approach in the 1980s and 1990s.

Today, a new generation of prominent pocket

cartoonists is at work including Nick Newman, Jeremy Banks (known as 'Banx'), Tim Sanders and Jonathan Pugh. The best-known practitioner of them all, though, is Matthew Pritchett. Better known as Matt, Pritchett started working for the *Daily Telegraph* in 1988 and since then has produced a front-page cartoon for the paper every day. In the process, not only has he become the highest-paid cartoonist in Britain, but he has also achieved the kind of status that most political cartoonists can only dream of: he has received multiple Cartoonist of the Year titles at the Press Awards for his work,

Matt at his desk in the *Daily Telegraph* offices where he produces his cartoon every day. 'I'm terrible on my own,' Matt has admitted. 'I'm very undisciplined and I need to be in an office surrounded by people and with the panic of having to get something done.'

as well as an MBE. It is hardly surprising that in the eyes of *Telegraph* readers, Matt overshadows his cartooning colleagues.

Many leading politicians over the last few years have claimed Matt to be their favourite political cartoonist, even though Matt has specifically stated that he does not consider himself to be one. Former prime minister John Major admired his 'gentle, understated humour'. Gordon Brown has said that 'If a picture can paint a thousand words, then a pocket cartoon conjured up by Matt can regularly do even more.' Theresa May thinks Matt is 'great' at taking major political events and seeing the humour in them: 'It's always good for politicians to laugh at ourselves and he helps us to do that.' Admittedly, not all political leaders have been such great fans. Former Labour leader Jeremy Corbyn was of the belief that none of the cartoons Matt had drawn about him were in the least bit funny, perhaps because they often portrayed him as bumbling and inept. But Corbyn is something of a lone voice. Matt's fan base even extends to royalty. Prince Philip, the late Duke of Edinburgh, called Matt a 'genius' for his 'ability to think of wonderfully appropriate swipes at the idiocies of contemporary life'.

Even if they have often been overshadowed by the great political cartoonists of the time, today's pocket cartoonists are consumed and adored by massive audiences including some of the most influential people in the country. However, a few pocket cartoonists worry that the very size and nature of a pocket cartoon means they are not fully appreciated by cartoon aficionados. Nick Newman, pocket cartoonist for the *Sunday Times*, argues that 'Pocket cartoons are treated less seriously, partly due to size, partly due to position [political cartoons are mostly located opposite the editorial] and partly due to portentousness of message.' Newman's position indicates a Napoleon-like concern that the diminutive size of pockets make them seem less noteworthy. However, many cartoonists have pointed out that there are significant benefits to drawing small-scale cartoons. Kathryn Lamb, pocket cartoonist for *Private Eye* and the *Spectator*, stoutly believes it is 'an advantage to do smaller drawings'.

Indeed, there can be no doubt that the size of the pocket cartoon gives it a certain upper hand over its political relative. Pocket cartoons naturally take much less time to draw, so the cartoonist can devote more time to coming up with ideas (or, as the *Independent*'s pocket cartoonist Tim Sanders jokingly sees it, time to 'get to the pub quicker'). Russel Herneman, cartoonist for *Private Eye*, among other publications, suggests that the pocket cartoonist gains from the hours freed up for 'the creative thinking process

"FOR YOUR BIRTHDAY I'VE SPLASHED OUT AND GOT US A POLITICAL CARTOON SPACE."

Pocket cartoonist James Whitworth pokes fun at his political cartooning colleagues for indulging in much more space to get their point across.

which can range from seconds to eons, within both genres'. Kipper Williams, who creates pocket cartoons for several publications including the *Spectator*, *Private Eye* and the *Critic*, says he prefers creating pocket cartoons to political ones as 'it's possible to cover a broader spread of topics and the relative speed of execution means you potentially get more bites of the cherry.' Osbert Lancaster once admitted that 'the cartoons only used to take about five minutes . . . no, maybe we'd better say fifteen – don't want to make it sound too easy!' This would have been an exasperating admission for the political cartoonist Sidney Strube, Lancaster's contemporary at the *Daily Express,* who spent on average five to eight hours a day producing a cartoon. This is how he recalled Lancaster's working practices to *Punch* cartoonist David Langdon:

> So I arrive each morning, sit meself [sic] down and start scratching my head for an idea . . . Then at about 11 o'clock, like clockwork, in comes the young feller [sic] Lancaster . . . After a few minutes he takes out a fountain pen of all things, scribbles a cartoon, gets up and walks to the editor's cubicle at the far end of the newsroom. There's a pause, followed by a loud guffaw. Lancaster emerges, tosses his piece of paper into an out-tray . . . And I sit at my drawing board sometimes to five o'clock in the ruddy evening.

Strube's frustration is understandable but arguably misplaced. Lancaster would most likely have spent hours beforehand thinking through his idea. In his younger days, he later confided, he would have done about eight roughs, seven of which would be rejected 'out of hand'. It's much the same for today's pocket cartoonists. They may not devote hours to producing the final item, but the preliminary stage may well have taken a considerable amount of time. Jonathan Pugh, who delivers seven or eight drafts for his editor at the *Daily Mail* every day, describes

the process as follows: 'I'll do rough drawings, which will be barely legible, with a caption underneath, which will give the editor an idea of what the cartoon might look like . . . The time-consuming bit is generally getting the caption right. The drawing I can get done in about half an hour.' Matt similarly takes up to a day to hit upon the right concept for his cartoon. He will arrive at the *Telegraph* around eight in the morning to look through all the papers to see what the main news stories are. Then he adopts what he calls 'a scattergun approach', noting down dozens of possible cartoon ideas before refining them into six or seven roughs. At four o'clock, he shows the results to his editor. As Matt admits, 'It's very rare that the first one gets through, and very often it's the very last one. I think of it as being a bit like colonic irrigation!'

If the mental effort that goes into a pocket cartoon is considerable, the speed at which it is then executed means that it involves less detail and technique than is the case for political cartoons. In any case, by their own admission, pocket cartoonists tend to be less artistically gifted than political or even strip cartoonists. Their fundamental skill, after all, lies in being funny day after day. Matt has admitted that he is 'not good at caricature and feet are impossible to draw'. He has acknowledged that he is heavily influenced by the drawing style of Bryan McAllister, a pocket cartoonist for the *Guardian*, who, according to political cartoonist Steve Bell, 'couldn't draw for toffees'. At his best, Osbert Lancaster was certainly a fine artist, but no pocket cartoonist since can really hold a candle to the great political cartoonists when it comes to artistic skill and execution. Among today's crop of pocket cartoonists it's hard to find any who match the impressive draughtsmanship of a Morten Morland, or a Peter Brookes, or a Dave Brown, or a Steve Bell. Mel Calman – one of the most successful and renowned practitioners of pocket cartooning – was, early on in his career, rejected by publication after publication because his draughtsmanship was deemed so poor. 'I rather doubt if "cartooning" (as it is generally called) is really your line,' the then art editor of *Punch*, Russell Brockbank, wrote in a rejection letter to Calman in 1956. 'Neither drawings nor ideas measure up to the standard required here I'm afraid.' Calman's lack of drawing ability ironically led directly to his future success as a pocket cartoonist. He developed a minimal style that Steve Bell has referred to as 'crude but exquisite'.

It appears that because of their limitations, pocket cartoonists feel more at home with the smaller format of pockets. Kathryn Lamb confides that she lacks the confidence to draw on a larger scale. 'I was naturally inclined to do smaller drawings,' she told me.

Jonathan Pugh has also admitted that 'anything much bigger and I'm drowning at sea'. In 1987, Nick Newman struggled when he stepped up to the larger-format cartoon to fill in temporarily for Wally Fawkes as the political cartoonist for the *London Daily News*. According to Newman, 'My very rare forays into serious "political" cartooning weren't very successful as I think I don't have the skill to make up for the lack of a joke with sublime artistry – which some "political" cartoonists use to great effect.'

To say that pocket cartoonists lack the 'sublime artistry' to fill a larger format is not in itself a criticism. Pocket cartoons are, after all, a form of shorthand. Their exponents must be able to convey an idea in a succinct, minimal way to fit the smaller space. One must also remember that it is the caption that is all-important to the pocket cartoon, so there is no requirement for it to be a masterpiece. In fact, Mel Calman believed that 90 per cent of his work lay in the caption. The opposite is true of political cartooning, which requires detailed and skilled drawing to get the idea across.

The focus on basic idea and caption highlights the essential way in which the purpose of pocket cartoons differs from that of political ones: they are there, quite simply, to amuse the reader. Nick Newman says, 'Political cartoonists can get away

"The Oprah interview's a terrible mistake- they should have gone with Emily Maitlis."

These cartoons, one pocket and one political, illustrate how the same story is depicted in different cartooning styles. The pocket cartoon (left) by Nick Newman, published in the *Sunday Times* on 7 March 2021, imagines Prince Andrew's reaction to Prince Harry and Meghan Markle's TV appearance following his own disastrous on-air interview with Emily Maitlis in 2019. Morten Morland's political cartoon from *The Times*, utilises the same joke but in a very different artistic style. 'Spot the difference . . . (apart from Morten's wonderful drawing and caricatures, obviously),' comments Newman.

with a beautiful drawing and a chin-stroking "joke" but the pocket cartoonist just has to be funny.' Jeremy Banks, pocket cartoonist for the *Financial Times*, the *Spectator* and many other publications, confirms the point: 'A pocket cartoon without the gag is nothing,' he argues. If there is a political agenda to a pocket cartoon, then it is very much a secondary consideration. Matt, for example, is clear that he is not interested in doing 'statement' cartoons, preferring to stick to jokes. Although the subject of his cartoons usually follows the main news story, as long as they are funny and vaguely topical then he finds his editor is happy. 'People tell me that my cartoons occasionally make political statements,' he says, 'but all I am going for is the cheap laugh.' If his cartoons do occasionally make a political point, then it's 'usually by mistake'. When pocket cartoons are political, they tend to be less interested in particular politicians than in how daily events affect ordinary people. According to Pugh, 'My cartoons have always been about everyday life. I was once asked to produce a daily cartoon on Iraq, but death and bombs aren't funny, so I focused on life's irritations – all that sand, machines not working and equipment shortages.' Matt describes his work in a similar vein as focusing on 'ordinary people affected by life'.

Political cartoons, by contrast, are strictly a medium for political comment. They focus on key events and the actions of the political elite, and their objective is to hold politicians to account through both humour and ridicule. Often this is achieved by either visual metaphor or by conflating two news stories. Pugh uses a cricket analogy to differentiate between political and pocket cartoons:

It's a bit like batting and bowling – same game, but a very different agenda. I like to think the purpose of the newspaper pocket cartoon is to cheer people up; a little oasis and light relief amid the daily gloom. The political cartoon is more about meaty hits into the solar plexus – sure, the odd light jab for a laugh – but it's there to express an opinion and get a point across, not simply to amuse.

Political cartoons are often very funny, but they do not have to be. In fact, humour can sometimes be inappropriate in a political cartoon if the subject matter is sober or tragic. Many political cartoons over the years have been serious. A prime example is a cartoon by Victor 'Vicky' Weisz published in the *News Chronicle* of 26 September 1950 following the coal mining disaster at Creswell Colliery. Entitled 'The Price of Coal', the cartoon depicts the families affected by an underground fire that killed 80 miners and makes a deeply serious point about workers' rights and the dangers of the mining industry.

So, is categorising cartoons useful or is it a complete irrelevance to most observers? Nick Newman, for one, thinks categorisation is largely meaningless. 'Categorisation helps aficionados and academics to pigeonhole cartoonists,' he says, 'but I think, for readers, cartoons are all one and the same . . . cartooning is just cartooning.' Russel

Published in September 1950 following the disaster at Creswell Colliery, Vicky's cartoon proves that the most impactful political cartoons do not have to be humorous.

between the different strands. There are, of course, pocket and political cartoons. There are social cartoons which lie somewhere in the middle; they intend to make the reader laugh but are drawn on a larger scale (Stan 'Mac' McMurtry and Paul Thomas come to mind). Then there are strip cartoons, which Kipper Williams thinks straddle all cartoon formats as they 'allow extra detail that wouldn't be so viable in a pocket cartoon' and which Steve Bell enjoys as 'you can do things at length and in more depth and you can be sillier and ruder.' Bell himself has drawn both political and strip cartoons for the *Guardian*. Paul Thomas has drawn political, social and pocket cartoons during his career. All of these cartoon forms can be equally enjoyed, but they are nevertheless clearly recognisable by their size and technique and can be distinguished by whether they set out to entertain or provoke. When it comes to editing books of cartoons, I believe it is indeed both necessary and more meaningful to categorise.

Herneman similarly argues that the only quality anyone cares about in any cartoon format is whether the cartoon is funny or not, and that any attempt to distinguish between genres 'owes more to semantics than politics'. I disagree. I am fascinated by the variety within the cartoon medium and I believe it is valuable to make distinctions

As to whether political cartoons are 'better' or more worthy of being singled out, opinions vary sharply. Some believe that pocket cartoons have a greater impact on readers because they deliver a joke rather than a political sermon. According to Thomas, 'Pockets are rarely as pompous as political ones where the cartoonist seeks to display his social conscience as a replacement for a clever

IT'S IMPORTANT TO SEE THE BIGGER PICTURE AND THE SMALLER ONE!

K.J.Lamb

Kathryn Lamb makes her case for the smaller-format, economically drawn pocket cartoon.

or funny idea.' Andy Davey, cartoonist for the *Independent*, *Telegraph* and *Evening Standard*, among others, believes 'A clever pocket cartoon can often do a better job at telling a political story than the overworked, self-righteous editorial cartoon.' Osbert Lancaster stated that his aim was not to preach or put over a particular political point of view, which he saw as a problem for the overtly political cartoonist. Political commentator Andrew Marr is of the opinion that Matt's influence has been greater than that of his political colleagues as he 'has dug himself into the consciousness of millions as few of his angrier, more flamboyant rivals have done'.

Champions of political cartoons, by contrast, point to those iconic works by Gillray, Low and Vicky, which have, over time, achieved a permanence in our collective memory. Political cartoons offer us an artistic visual commentary that vividly documents our political and social world in incredibly creative and witty ways. The smaller-format, quick-fix pocket cartoons are brilliantly funny but they can only offer a snapshot of the contemporary scene and, unlike political cartoons, pockets can lose their meaning as humour changes through the years. By contrast, the political cartoonist's perspective on the body politic can become a valuable historical resource to tap into in order to recall the varying perspectives and nuances of that time. That is why I have always championed them. We are fortunate enough to be living at a time when both pocket and political cartoons are thriving – to the daily delight of millions of newspaper readers up and down the country. But I hope that as you browse through this latest collection of political cartoons you recognise them for the valuable, artistic and thought-provoking records of an extraordinary 12 months in British history that I believe them to be.

THE CARTOONS

IMPUNITY
PUTIN

World leaders demanded answers from Vladimir Putin after toxicology examinations showed that the Russian opposition leader, Alexei Navalny, had been poisoned with a Novichok nerve agent. Navalny has long been the prominent face of opposition to Putin, denouncing the president's party as a place of 'crooks and thieves'. German Chancellor Angela Merkel said the attempted murder raised 'very difficult questions that only the Russian government can answer'. A Kremlin spokesperson retorted that the accusations were 'empty noise' and 'We do not intend to take it seriously.'

4 September 2020
Nicola Jennings
Guardian

While on the campaign trail, Donald Trump repeatedly claimed that the postal voting system was vulnerable to fraud and that his Democratic opponents could steal the election by manipulating postal ballots. However, at an event in North Carolina, Trump encouraged supporters to vote twice, both by post and in person. North Carolina's attorney general tweeted that the president had 'outrageously encouraged' people in the state 'to break the law in order to help him sow chaos'. Trump's opponent, Joe Biden, had supported the expansion of postal voting to make it safer to vote during the coronavirus pandemic.

4 September 2020
Dave Brown
Independent

7 September 2020
Patrick Blower
Telegraph

Extinction Rebellion protestors halted the distribution of major newspapers by blockading the entrance to three printworks owned by Rupert Murdoch. The *Telegraph*, the *Sun* and *The Times* were some of the newspapers affected. Demonstrators accused Murdoch's media outlets of failing to properly report on climate change. The protestors chained themselves to bamboo towers and used vehicles adorned with the phrases 'Free the truth' and 'Five Crooks Control our News' to block roads.

EU leaders said they had lost trust in Boris Johnson after he signalled that he intended to break international law by overriding key elements of the Brexit treaty. The Internal Market Bill was set to 'eliminate the legal force of parts of the withdrawal agreement' in key areas, including the painstakingly negotiated agreement on Northern Ireland. President of the European Commission, Ursula von der Leyen, said that the plans 'would break international law and undermine trust', while Charles Michel, president of the European Council, described the move as 'unacceptable'.

10 September 2020
Steven Camley
Herald Scotland

'Operation Moonshot' was Boris Johnson's ambitious plan to process millions of coronavirus tests every day. Experts expressed concern over laboratory capacity for processing tests while technology for more rapid tests 'does not, as yet, exist'. Leaked documents estimated the plan could cost £100 billion, which is equivalent to the UK's entire education budget. During the EU referendum, Johnson famously campaigned alongside a red bus emblazoned with the words 'We send the EU £350 million a week, let's fund our NHS instead' – a claim that the UK Statistics Authority later called 'potentially misleading'.

11 September 2020
Morten Morland
The Times

BACON SANDWICH...

During a heated House of Commons debate, former leader of the Labour Party, Ed Miliband, tore into Boris Johnson's proposed Internal Market Bill. Miliband accused Johnson of not having read or understood the bill and called it 'legislative hooliganism'. The prime minister declined to answer questions. *Guardian* columnist John Crace called the speech an 'evisceration' and wrote that Miliband 'comprehensively ripped Boris Johnson's facile and fraudulent arguments to shreds'. The cartoon recalls Miliband being ridiculed for awkwardly eating a bacon sandwich in 2014.

16 September 2020
Dave Brown
Independent

According to the cartoonist, 'The government had published new coronavirus rules and contradictions. The latest fiasco was that you couldn't meet another family in the park for a picnic, but grouse shooting was deemed to be perfectly acceptable.' From 14 September, the 'rule of six' law came into effect, limiting the number of people who could meet from different households. Several sports and activities were exempt including hunting and shooting. Shadow Environment Secretary Luke Pollard commented, 'The Conservatives are distracted with trying to exempt the bloodsport passions of their big donors.'

16 September 2020
Peter Brookes
The Times

After a sharp rise in coronavirus cases, local restrictions were introduced in North East England. These included a 10pm curfew and a ban on mixing with other households. Northumberland, North Tyneside, South Tyneside, Newcastle upon Tyne, Gateshead, Sunderland and County Durham were all affected. Boris Johnson stated, 'The only way to make sure the country is able to enjoy Christmas is to be tough now.' Earlier in the year, Dominic Cummings came under fire for driving to Barnard Castle in County Durham, supposedly to test his eyesight, in violation of the stay-at-home rule.

18 September 2020
Steve Bell
Guardian

Boris Johnson was forced to admit that the Test and Trace operation was not 'ideal', despite having promised a 'world-beating' system four months previously. Hospital staff complained that they were forced to stay away from work for days as they waited to receive results and had to travel long distances for tests – one GP, based in Margate, was told to travel 266 miles to Leeds to be tested. Labour leader Sir Keir Starmer warned that the Test and Trace system was 'on the verge of collapse'. In addition, the prime minister revealed that it was now 'absolutely inevitable' that the UK was entering the second wave of the coronavirus pandemic, with new cases doubling in a week.

20 September 2020
Chris Riddell
Observer

After the 'rule of six' law came into effect, Policing Minister Kit Malthouse said people should report their neighbours if they were violating the rule. Police could issue fines of £3,200 to people caught breaking the law in an effort to limit the spread of coronavirus. The new measures came into force as 6,000 new cases per day were recorded in England. The government's scientific advisors warned that, by November, new cases could rise to 50,000 per day unless drastic actions were taken.

21 September 2020
Patrick Blower
Telegraph

On 22 September, Boris Johnson announced sweeping new lockdown restrictions. These included a curfew for pubs and restaurants, fines for people failing to wears masks and advice to work from home. 'We have reached a perilous turning point,' Johnson said. 'This is the moment when we must act.' The prime minister said that the selected measures would quickly reduce the spread of the virus while causing 'the minimum damage to lives and livelihoods'. Even so, Carolyn Fairbairn, director-general of the Confederation of British Industry, said there was 'no avoiding the crushing blow new measures bring for thousands of firms'.

23 September 2020
Christian Adams
Evening Standard

Donald Trump and Joe Biden prepared to face each other in their first presidential debate in Ohio. The death toll from coronavirus had just topped 200,000 in the United States – by far the highest in the world. Trump insisted his administration had prevented that number being 'substantially more'. However, the president had been heavily criticised throughout the pandemic for voicing unproven facts about the virus, recommending dangerous treatments, complaining that too much testing was making the US look bad and refusing to wear a face mask.

25 September 2020
Kevin Kallaugher
Economist

The furlough scheme came to earth with a bump as Chancellor Rishi Sunak unveiled new measures to protect jobs. Under the new Job Support Scheme the government would continue to top up wages, but the government's contribution would fall sharply – it would cover 22 per cent of a monthly wage as opposed to 80 per cent under the furlough scheme. 'The primary goal of our economic policy remains unchanged – to support people's jobs – but the way we achieve that must evolve,' Sunak said. Meanwhile, a Brexit agreement hung in the balance as UK and EU negotiators met for new rounds of talks, with no-deal seen as a strong possibility.

27 September 2020
Chris Riddell
Observer

'Well, we'll have to see what happens,' Donald Trump responded when asked if he would commit to a peaceful transfer of power following the US election. He also said that the result could end up in the Supreme Court and cast further doubts on the postal voting system. According to the cartoonist, 'Comparing a current politician to a Nazi can be a dangerous game, not least because we might get censored by our editors. And there is a danger that the comparison could undermine the extremely harsh judgement that the Nazis deserve. With a little allowance made for cartoonist's hyperbole this worked for me.'

27 September 2020
Peter Schrank
The Times

BREAKING BBC NEWS
GOVERNMENT BEGINS SHAKE-UP OF THE BBC

28 September 2020
Ben Jennings
Guardian

A *Times* report quoted an anonymous BBC insider who claimed that the government was waging 'all out war' against the broadcaster. The article was published amid reports that the right-wing former *Daily Telegraph* editor, Charles Moore, was the government's pick to be the next chairman of the BBC. Moore is known to be deeply critical of the broadcaster and was once taken to court for refusing to pay his licence fee. A former employee of Moore's said that Moore would 'gut the BBC, perhaps getting his revenge for its treatment of Thatcher'.

A *New York Times* investigation revealed that President Donald Trump paid only $750 in federal tax in 2016, the year he was elected. It also revealed that he had paid no income tax in ten of the previous 15 years, despite earning $427.4 million in 2018 and being worth an estimated $2.1 billion. Trump has repeatedly refused to make his tax records public and has fought legal efforts to compel him to do so by claiming he was undergoing an audit.

28 September 2020
Christian Adams
Evening Standard

1 October 2020
Steve Bell
Guardian

During the first presidential debate Donald Trump failed to condemn the actions of the Proud Boys, a group which the Anti-Defamation League has categorised as a violent, nationalistic, Islamophobic and misogynistic hate group. When asked if he would denounce white supremacists, Trump replied that the Proud Boys should 'stand back and stand by'. Many in the group took this as tacit approval and made the phrase 'Stand Back, Stand By' part of their logo. Later Trump claimed that he did not know who the Proud Boys were.

Former Labour leader Jeremy Corbyn apologised after he was photographed having dinner with eight other people, therefore breaking the law on the 'rule of six'. The week before, the new Labour leader, Sir Keir Starmer, had delivered a speech at the party's conference in Doncaster in which he made it clear that he was breaking with Corbyn's politics. 'This is a party under new leadership,' Starmer emphasised. 'It's time to get serious about winning.'

1 October 2020
Christian Adams
Evening Standard

CLOSE CONTACTS...

COVID IS A HOAX

COVID-19 TESTING AREA

Ben Jennings

4 October 2020
Ben Jennings
Guardian

On 2 October, President Donald Trump confirmed that he had tested positive for coronavirus and was transported to hospital for treatment. The president's supporters gathered outside with placards and flowers. Three days later, Trump made an impromptu appearance, waving to the crowd from an SUV. Concerns were raised about the other people in the vehicle, given that Trump was contagious. The president tested positive the night after a campaign event in New Jersey with 206 attendees: officials had to scramble to inform everyone in attendance of their possible exposure to the virus.

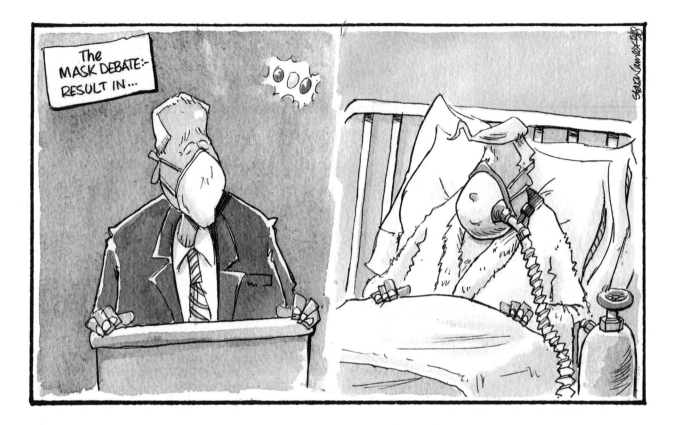

Throughout the pandemic, Donald Trump had ignored the advice of medical experts, particularly when refusing to wear a mask – a precaution public health officials advised could save thousands of lives. Only two days before his coronavirus diagnosis, the president had mocked Joe Biden during the presidential debate saying, 'Every time you see him, he's got a mask. He could be speaking 200 feet away from it, and he shows up with the biggest mask I've seen.' Later Biden commented that he was unsurprised that the president has caught the virus, retorting 'Masks matter.'

5 October 2020
Steven Camley
Herald Scotland

In an upbeat speech at the virtual Conservative Party conference, Boris Johnson vowed to defeat coronavirus and build a better nation. Johnson said that the 'ructions' caused by the pandemic would lead to the UK being transformed by 2030, including mass home ownership, more electric vehicles and blue passports. According to Johnson, the UK would be 'the greatest place on Earth'. He did warn that the government intended to significantly roll back the economic support it had offered during the pandemic, saying 'we Conservatives believe that way lies disaster.'

7 October 2020
Patrick Blower
Telegraph

According to the cartoonist, 'There was a great moment during the vice-presidential debate when a fly landed on Mike Pence's hair. It lingered there for an agonisingly long two minutes. It's the story of Pence really – the fly got more attention than he ever would in a whole year. It worked with the fly being Trump, who was out of hospital and telling the world he felt "perfect" after having coronavirus.'

9 October 2020
Peter Brookes
The Times

12 October 2020
Brian Adcock
Independent

On 12 October, the prime minister announced a three-tiered system of coronavirus alerts in England. Northern cities such as Liverpool, Manchester and Newcastle were thought to be the most at-risk. In areas labelled 'very high' risk, pubs, bars, casinos and gyms were asked to close and the chancellor pledged to pay two-thirds of hospitality workers' wages. However, mayor of Greater Manchester, Andy Burnham, protested that 'To accept the chancellor's package would be to surrender our residents to hardship and our businesses to failure.'

Newly released documents revealed that SAGE, the government's scientific advisors, had called for an urgent two-week lockdown a month earlier. The report, dated 21 September 2020, warned that the country faced a 'very large epidemic with catastrophic consequences' unless the government imposed an immediate circuit-breaker lockdown. SAGE also recommended other measures but only one, issuing advice to work from home, had been introduced. The latest figures showed that the pandemic was now doubling in size every week.

14 October 2020
Dave Brown
Independent

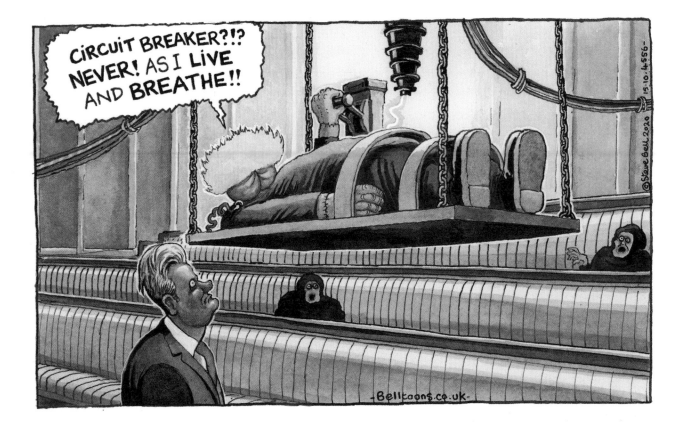

15 October 2020
Steve Bell
Guardian

Following the publication of the SAGE report, Sir Keir Starmer called for a two- or three-week circuit-breaker lockdown to curb the spread of coronavirus. The Labour leader said that the government had 'lost control' and warned that the UK would 'sleepwalk into a long and bleak winter'. In response, the prime minister accused Starmer of opportunism and defended the tier system, insisting that no one wanted the 'disaster' of a second lockdown.

With less than three months to go until the UK was due to leave the single market, fishing rights became a key sticking point in negotiating a trade deal. French President Emmanuel Macron issued a firm statement on fishing rights in the English Channel, declaring, 'Under no circumstance will our fishermen be the ones sacrificed for this Brexit. We did not choose Brexit; it's the choice of the British people.' A quarter of France's national catch comes from British waters – France had pushed back against any change to the existing arrangements.

17 October 2020
Peter Brookes
The Times

19 October 2020
Nicola Jennings
Guardian

Leaders in Greater Manchester, including Mayor Andy Burnham, rejected a move to place the region into the top tier alert level without better support. The government had offered Greater Manchester a financial package worth tens of millions but local leaders criticised the support on offer, calculating that there was a £62 million gap between the money offered and the necessary level of support. Michael Gove accused local political leaders of opting for 'press conferences and posturing' over saving lives.

According to the cartoonist, 'The exemplary Manchester United footballer, Marcus Rashford, had expressed his disappointment and frustration about the government's refusal to budge on holiday meal support for kids. The idea of Boris Johnson as the fat beadle was irresistible – unyielding as Oliver Twist (Rashford) holds up several empty bowls and points to a bunch of sad looking kids at a table in the Victorian-style poorhouse. The composition is a nod to George Cruikshank's illustration of Dickens's tale.'

22 October 2020
Andy Davey
Evening Standard

24 October 2020
Kevin Kallaugher
Economist

Pope Francis expressed his support for same-sex civil unions for the first time in his papacy. 'Homosexual people have a right to be in a family. They are children of God . . . What we have to create is a civil union law. That way they are legally covered,' he stated. Pope Francis also endorsed legal protection for the rights of gay couples when he was the archbishop of Buenos Aires. The comments angered many conservative Catholics who already oppose the Pope's more progressive views on divorce and capitalism.

Donald Trump spent much of his presidential campaign discouraging supporters from voting by post, effectively suppressing his own party's turnout – early estimates indicated that just 26.1 per cent of early voters were Republican. Joe Biden, on the other hand, had encouraged supporters to vote by post during the pandemic, leading to a historic number of postal ballots. The Democrats' early-vote advantage was pronounced in the key swing states of Florida, North Carolina and Pennsylvania. Meanwhile, a new rule for the second debate meant that the candidates' microphones were muted while their opponent was speaking to prevent the two men from interrupting one another.

25 October 2020
Chris Riddell
Observer

Resistance to coronavirus restrictions began to show as more areas of the UK were moved into the highest tier of lockdown restrictions. Maureen Eames from Barnsley went viral after she told reporters, 'I'm 83, I don't give a sod . . . I'm not gonna be fastened in a house.' In Bangor, Gwilym Owen was filmed tearing plastic sheets and prohibition tape from non-essential items in Tesco. The Welsh government had imposed a two-week 'firebreak' lockdown and, under the rules, supermarkets were prevented from selling non-essential items such as clothing and electrical goods.

26 October 2020
Steve Bright
Sun

"Oh, for heaven's sake – wear a mask ... don't wear a mask!"

The Scottish government told people to celebrate Halloween at home instead of going trick-or-treating as the cases of coronavirus continued to rise. Deputy First Minister John Swinney advised against guising – dressing up and going door-to-door – saying it 'brings an additional and avoidable risk of spreading the virus, our clear advice for families is to avoid it.' He also warned that bags of sweets could be 'purveyors of coronavirus'.

27 October 2020
Steven Camley
Herald Scotland

27 October 2020
Christian Adams
Evening Standard

Boris Johnson could lose his advantage in many of the new Conservative seats that won him the last election, a report concluded. 'Red wall' constituencies – those that historically supported the Labour Party – would be disproportionately affected by Brexit because they rely heavily on manufacturing and might, therefore, be likely to switch allegiances. In addition, 54 Conservative MPs who represent 'red wall' constituencies wrote to the prime minister to demand payback for lockdowns affecting the North and to urge him to fulfil his promise to 'level up' Britain. Many saw this demand as a dangerous sign for the prime minister.

Former president Barack Obama slammed Donald Trump for being 'jealous of Covid's media coverage' and ridiculed his successor's response to the pandemic. Appearing at a rally in support of Joe Biden, Obama asked the crowd, 'What is his closing argument? That people are too focused on Covid . . . He said this at one of his rallies, "Covid, Covid, Covid".' In an evisceration of Trump's character, Obama accused him of being 'incapable of taking the job seriously' and of not showing 'any interest in doing the work, or helping anybody but himself and his friends'.

29 October 2020
Steve Bell
Guardian

The former Labour leader, Jeremy Corbyn, was suspended from the party after a damning human rights report found 'serious failings' in how antisemitism was dealt with under his leadership. Corbyn issued a statement saying that, while he condemned antisemitism, the scale of the problem had been 'dramatically overstated for political reasons'. That comment drew a swift response from the Labour Party, who suspended Corbyn pending an investigation. Sir Keir Starmer retorted that those who said the problem was 'exaggerated' were 'part of the problem and . . . should be nowhere near the Labour Party'.

1 November 2020
Morten Morland
The Times

According to the cartoonist, 'Donald Trump was busying himself after polling day, in the dying moments of his imperial glory, by rubbishing the American democratic system itself. In states where he was gaining ground, he demanded the count to continue, in states where his lead was faltering, he demanded it stop. He rubbished the counters, the checking system, the FBI, anyone who was around. A pathetic end to a narcissist. To miss an opportunity to use that great old Frank Muir/Denis Norden gag would be unforgivable, so here it is again. It was famously cried out by Kenneth Williams as Julius Caesar in *Carry on Cleo*.'

6 November 2020
Andy Davey
Telegraph

On 7 November, the US media finally declared that Joe Biden would become the 46th President of the United States. Donald Trump had held a lead on election night but as officials counted hundreds of thousands of postal votes over several days, it became clear that the result had swung dramatically in Biden's favour. During the tense count, Trump had attempted to undermine election officials by falsely claiming the election was being stolen and he launched lawsuits to stop vote counting. During one press conference, media outlets even had to mute Trump because of his false and outlandish claims about fraudulent voting.

9 November 2020
Morten Morland
The Times

Boris Johnson's close advisor and director of communications, Lee Cain, quit after reports of a bitter power struggle at Number 10. There had allegedly been arguments over plans to make Cain the prime minister's chief of staff, leading to speculation that Dominic Cummings might quit in protest. Cain had previously been a tabloid reporter where his claim to fame was dressing as a chicken and pursuing David Cameron during the 2010 election campaign.

13 November 2020
Steve Bell
Guardian

14 November 2020
Steven Camley
Herald Scotland

Boris Johnson said that he had an 'excellent conversation' with Joe Biden following his election win and that they had many areas of 'common cause'. However, insiders claimed that Biden had been stern on the issue of Brexit and warned against breaching the Good Friday Agreement. Meanwhile, Number 10 sources claimed that the prime minister's then-fiancée, Carrie Symonds, had engineered the departure of Lee Cain and was pushing for the removal of Johnson's 'Brexit Boys'. 'Few if any prime ministerial spouses have been so . . . apparently powerful,' wrote the *Daily Mail*'s David Wilcock.

PLAYTIME OVER...

Dominic Cummings was sacked from his role as the prime minister's top aide after an alleged showdown with Carrie Symonds. Newspapers reported that the two had disagreed over the appointment of Allegra Stratton as Number 10's new spokesperson as well as Symonds's distaste for Johnson's 'blokey' inner circle. The incident lead to a bitter rumour war in which it was claimed that Symonds called Johnson more than 20 times a day and that she had been given the nickname Princess Nut Nuts.

15 November 2020
Morten Morland
The Times

The Trump administration condemned China's 'unjustified use of force' in Hong Kong as police laid siege to a university campus with hundreds of protesters inside. The escalating conflict stemmed from plans to extradite 'criminals' to China and from the Chinese state's increasing control over Hong Kong. Meanwhile, Donald Trump still refused to concede the presidential election and was pursuing lawsuits to prevent the certification of results. His supporters gathered for protests in Washington D.C. where 20 people were arrested for assault and weapons possession. One stabbing was reported and two police officers were injured.

20 November 2020
Kevin Kallaugher
Economist

The Labour Party's national executive committee lifted the suspension of Jeremy Corbyn's membership after he issued a statement 'clarifying' his controversial remarks that antisemitism in the party had been exaggerated. However, Sir Keir Starmer sparked a furious response from some MPs after he refused to restore the whip and admit Corbyn as a Labour MP, arguing that Corbyn had 'undermined' trust in the party. Corbyn's supporters argued that he was being 'persecuted' and Unite union leader Len McCluskey described the move as 'a witch hunt'.

20 November 2020
Peter Brookes
The Times

Text on tank: We spend £15bn on Overseas Aid let's just vaporise Johnny Foreigner instead ☠ Vote Defence Budget

20 November 2020
Dave Brown
Independent

Nearly 200 charities and aid organisations called on the prime minister to reconsider after it was revealed that Britain's overseas aid spending would be reduced by billions of pounds to just 0.5 per cent of GDP. Speaking in a Commons debate, Boris Johnson refused to commit to maintaining international aid spending but did unveil a four-year £16.5 billion boost to the defence budget. Johnson said the additional defence spending would allow the military to invest in new technology and added, 'There is absolutely no relation to discussions about overseas aid.'

Priti Patel came under fire after a report concluded that she broke the ministerial code by failing to treat her staff at the Home Office 'with consideration and respect'. However, as the sole arbiter of the rules, Boris Johnson decided that there had been no breach of code and allowed Patel to keep her job. According to the cartoonist, 'A report into the behaviour of Priti Patel had found that she had "unintentionally" bulldozed her staff. Johnson was digging in and refusing to fire her. His problem is that he's unintentionally useless.'

21 November 2020
Peter Brookes
The Times

TRUMP'S LAST STAND

21 November 2020
Ingram Pinn
Financial Times

Thousands of Donald Trump's supporters gathered in Washington D.C. to back his unsubstantiated claims of election fraud, with crowds chanting 'Four more years!' The event went by several names, including Stop the Steal D.C. There were reports of clashes between the marchers and counter-protestors resulting in numerous arrests and minor injuries. Many members of the Proud Boys were seen on the streets clad in black and wearing ballistic vests. Trump called the support 'heartwarming'.

The National Audit Office found that the government had prioritised companies recommended by MPs and peers when purchasing personal protective equipment. Over half of the £18 billion spent on contracts was awarded without competitive tender and, in some cases, key documentation was missing. The government also hired Dido Harding and Kate Bingham, both wives of Conservative ministers, as Test and Trace chief and head of the UK Vaccine Taskforce respectively. The *British Medical Journal* said that the government had 'unleashed state corruption on a grand scale'. The cartoon is inspired by James Gillray's 'The Plumb-pudding in Danger', which depicts Napoleon and William Pitt the Younger carving up the globe.

23 November 2020
Ben Jennings
Guardian

THE HAND OF RISH

'Our economic emergency has only just begun,' claimed Rishi Sunak in his spending review. He revealed that the government had so far spent £280 billion on coronavirus relief but the economy was set to contract by 11.3 per cent, the largest decline in three centuries. In response, the chancellor announced that there would be a pay freeze for all public sector workers, except for medical NHS staff, and it was reported that significant tax rises might be necessary. In other news, Argentinian football legend Diego Maradona died at the age of 60. He was famous for his 'Hand of God' goal that eliminated England from the 1986 World Cup, despite many claiming he had cheated.

26 November 2020
Christian Adams
Evening Standard

Negotiations between the UK and EU resumed as both sides raced to reach a Brexit deal before the December deadline. EU chief negotiator Michel Barnier said that the 'same significant differences persist', while Boris Johnson reiterated that there remained 'substantial and important differences'. Meanwhile, Michael Gove warned that England's hospitals could be 'overwhelmed' unless tougher restrictions to fight the spread of coronavirus came into force. The UK death toll had reached 58,030, with 15,871 positive cases recorded in 24 hours.

29 November 2020
Chris Riddell
Observer

29 November 2020
Morten Morland
The Times

Executives from Britain's major pub groups wrote to Boris Johnson asking him to save the industry from the 'darkest of moments,' claiming that 'The pub is clearly being singled out for exceptionally harsh and unjustified treatment.' The plea came as a stricter tier system saw 99 per cent of England enter the highest two tiers, with tight restrictions on bars and restaurants and a ban on mixing indoors. A report by the Office for National Statistics revealed that over a third of hospitality firms had little or no confidence in surviving the next three months.

Following a national lockdown in November 2020, the prime minister announced that non-essential shops would be able to reopen and remain open for 24 hours a day in the run up to Christmas. However, the Centre for Retail Research estimated that around 125,000 retail jobs had already been lost in the first eight months of the year, with 13,867 shops shutting permanently. The British Retail Consortium estimated that shops had lost £8 billion in November alone.

1 December 2020
Graeme Bandeira
Yorkshire Post

England entered a new regional system of restrictions from 2 December. Under the Tier Two restrictions, pubs and restaurants would be able to reopen only if they offered a 'substantial meal'. Michael Gove got into a spot of bother after he stated on *Good Morning Britain* that a scotch egg was probably only a starter, but after his colleague George Eustice told LBC that a scotch egg would count as a proper meal, Gove had to perform a U-turn. Businesses faced fines of £10,000 or even closure if they failed to comply with the regulations.

2 December 2020
Peter Brookes
The Times

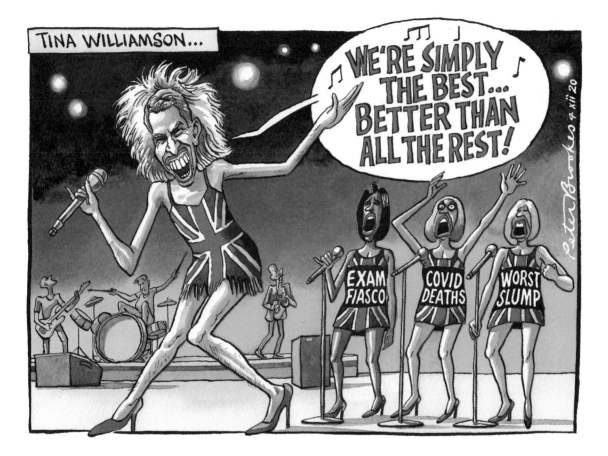

The UK became the first country to approve the Pfizer-BioNTech coronavirus vaccine on 2 December, paving way for the vaccine rollout the following week. Controversially, Education Secretary Gavin Williamson said that the UK had authorised the vaccine faster than France, Belgium and the US because the UK was a 'much better country'. According to the cartoonist, 'Williamson had said the UK was a better country than all others – basically another cabinet minister making another blooper . . . People said he was making a joke, but he shouldn't have been joking. The backing singers say it all.'

4 December 2020
Peter Brookes
The Times

UK and EU negotiators entered a crucial stage of Brexit talks, with the two sides remaining in a deadlock over fishing rights. The UK government lowered its demands by asking EU fishermen to hand over up to 60 per cent of the value of fish caught in British waters. This was still very far from the 15 to 18 per cent of the value of stock that the EU had offered. Number 10 dismissed that figure as 'derisory'. The cartoon mirrors the Mexican standoff scene in Quentin Tarantino's film *Reservoir Dogs*.

5 December 2020
Ben Jennings
Guardian

With time running out to reach a Brexit deal, Boris Johnson flew to Brussels to meet with the president of the European Commission, Ursula von der Leyen. The pair talked through the major sticking points – fishing rights, competition rights, and how the deal would be policed – over dinner. Meanwhile, Tony Schwartz, the co-author of Donald Trump's book *The Art of the Deal*, called the president a 'sociopath' who would be 'inflicting suffering on us all' in his last weeks in office. Schwartz had previously said that the book is his 'greatest regret in life' and that it should be 'recategorized as fiction'.

10 December 2020
Steven Camley
Herald Scotland

'LET'S GIVE IT A MISS – THE STREETS ARE PAVED WITH FACE MASKS AND ALL THE PUBS ARE SHUT'

16 December 2020
Paul Thomas
Daily Mail

London returned to a strict lockdown after moving into Tier Three or 'very high alert'. Under the Tier Three restrictions all hospitality venues, including pubs and restaurants, were to close, residents were prevented from meeting indoors or outdoors and people were asked not to travel to the area. Mayor of London, Sadiq Khan, said the decision was 'incredibly disappointing for businesses' but that it was 'clear that the virus is accelerating'.

Jacob Rees-Mogg was branded 'Scrooge' after he remarked that Unicef should be 'ashamed of itself' for 'playing politics' by providing free breakfasts to children in deprived parts of London. Neil Coyle MP offered to be the 'Spirit of Christmas Present' by inviting Rees-Mogg to a site supporting children in Southwark in order to 'prevent the ghastly spectacle of suggesting those who help children in need "should be ashamed" in the run up to Christmas.'

19 December 2020
Dave Brown
Independent

According to the cartoonist, 'Fears of a "Lockdown 3" were rampant as the virus took hold under the guise of a new variant. Christmas looked in danger of being hijacked by the Grinch but Boris Johnson – always wanting to present good news – resisted until the last minute. In the end it wasn't called lockdown – he simply added another tier to half the country, thereby retaining his benevolent Santa disguise.'

20 December 2020
Andy Davey
Telegraph

Sir Keir Starmer announced that Labour was establishing a commission to accelerate the redistribution of wealth, power and opportunity across the UK, claiming it was 'the boldest devolution project in a generation'. Starmer said that the pandemic had put 'rocket boosters' under the case for decentralisation. In Scotland, the commission's aim was to offer a third way between independence and the status quo. However, polling indicated that 58 per cent of Scottish people were already in support of independence.

22 December 2020
Morten Morland
The Times

22 December 2020
Paul Thomas
Daily Mail

Almost 3,000 lorries became stuck at UK ports after France shut its border with the UK for 48 hours amid fears of a new coronavirus variant first detected in Kent. France and other EU member states were calling for hauliers to be tested for coronavirus before entering their countries. Huge queues had also been reported in previous days as companies stock-piled goods in order to avoid Brexit disruption. Operation Stack was implemented on the coast-bound M20 motorway.

According to the cartoonist, 'Occasionally, when there's room or if I ask *really* nicely, Ted [the editor] will let me put a political-shaped cartoon in the *Metro*. This one is about the stumbling block of Brexit and pet passports over the Christmas period. When the opportunity arises I'll often pop in characters from other cartoonists' work as a kind of nod . . . Holding the anchor we have Grandma from Giles, an early influence on me, and behind her holding the anvil is Gustav Bird from Tintin's *The Secret of the Unicorn*.'

23 December 2020
Guy Venables
Metro

25 December 2020
Patrick Blower
Telegraph

Scientific data showed that the coronavirus was spreading exponentially in London and parts of the South East so, on 19 December, Boris Johnson announced that the affected areas would be placed into a new Tier Four. Those in Tier Four were told to stay at home and not to leave the area. The announcement sparked a flood of people trying to leave the capital before the rules came into effect in order to be with their families at Christmas. Police forces said that they were prepared to fine people flouting the rules and were stepping up visibility to deter people from leaving their homes.

On Christmas Eve, Boris Johnson announced that the EU and UK had reached a post-Brexit trade deal, just a week before the deadline. Johnson claimed that it was 'a good deal for the whole of Europe' but acknowledged that compromises had been made – the EU's share of fish caught in British waters was only cut by 25 per cent. Representatives of the fishing industry accused the government of 'caving in' and making 'significant concessions'. Andrew Locker of Lockers Trawlers said, 'I'm angry, disappointed and betrayed.'

28 December 2020
David Simonds
Guardian

The former foreign secretary, Jeremy Hunt, accused the government of failing to protect British Iranian nationals held in Iran, including Nazanin Zaghari-Ratcliffe. Hunt argued that not enough was being done to find a way around US and EU sanctions to pay the £400 million debt the UK owes Iran, one of the main barriers to the release of dual nationals. According to the cartoonist, 'This is an important story that I had wanted to comment on for some time. Not only because of the personal tragedy involved, but also because it exposes the limits of British power. The grandiose words on the inside cover of our British passports don't amount to much anymore.'

29 December 2020
Peter Schrank
The Times

Health Secretary Matt Hancock said the NHS was facing 'unprecedented pressures' as record numbers of coronavirus cases were reported. On 29 December, the UK recorded 53,135 new coronavirus cases as well as 414 deaths. Dr Susan Hopkins, senior advisor at Public Health England, said that the surge in cases was of 'extreme concern, particularly as our hospitals are at their most vulnerable.' The government had relaxed social distancing restrictions for Christmas Day, with people from three households not in Tier Four allowed to celebrate together.

30 December 2020
Brian Adcock
Independent

TIME'S UP

EXAM PAPERS 2021

2 January 2021
Nicola Jennings
Guardian

Education Secretary Gavin Williamson confirmed that pupils would 'absolutely' sit their exams as planned despite delays to the school term. Due to a new surge in coronavirus cases, the government announced that students taking exams that year would not go back to school until 11 January, with all other pupils due back on 18 January. Williamson said he was 'absolutely confident' that there would be no more delays, although teaching unions accused the government of 'another last-minute mess'.

On 4 January, Boris Johnson announced that England would enter another national lockdown. A more transmissible variant of coronavirus had caused a huge rise in cases with over 30 per cent more patients in hospital than the week before. People were once more asked to stay at home. All schools were closed. Leader of the Liberal Democrats, Ed Davey, accused the prime minister of making a habit of responding late to the scientific advice: 'He was late on the first [lockdown], he was late on the second, late on the third and that's because he ignores the advice of experts.'

6 January 2021
Peter Brookes
The Times

Hundreds of Donald Trump's supporters stormed the US Capitol building on 6 January. The building was vandalised, offices ransacked, police officers were beaten and four people died. Earlier in the day, Trump had addressed a 'Save America' rally at which he urged his supporters to march on Capitol Hill where Congress was meeting to certify Joe Biden's election victory. Members of Congress and staffers had to cower under seats and hide in offices as shots rang out.

8 January 2021
Graeme Bandeira
Yorkshire Post

According to the cartoonist, 'The official police advice on how to deal with people [breaking] lockdown was summarised as "Engage, Explain, Encourage, Enforce". Priti Patel said officers "will not hesitate to enforce" Covid lockdown rules. She could not wait to get stuck in. Matt Hancock, our own Sergeant Dixon of Dock Green, wanted to "engage" – supporting fines and a good talking to. Mind how you go.'

11 January 2021
Andy Davey
Telegraph

Boris Johnson was criticised after he was spotted cycling in the Olympic Park, seven miles from his home, even though government advice was to stay within your local area. A Number 10 source said that Johnson was operating within the rules, as they did not specifically prohibit driving short distances to take exercise. The source refused to confirm whether the prime minister had driven there. Labour MP Andy Slaughter commented, 'Once again it is do as I say not as I do from the prime minister.'

13 January 2021
Peter Brookes
The Times

Scottish fishermen were forced to sail to Denmark to sell their catch after prices in the UK collapsed following Brexit. Purchasers were turning to other markets as red tape meant that fish purchased in the UK was rotting by the time it reached European customers. Meanwhile, images circulated online of the meagre food parcels sent to children who qualified for free school meals during lockdown. Some parcels contained only a few items worth £5 when they were supposed to contain food to the value of £30 and last for 10 days. Education Secretary Gavin Williamson said that the images were 'absolutely disgusting' and that schools would be able to offer food vouchers instead.

15 January 2021
Steven Camley
Herald Scotland

17 January 2021
Morten Morland
The Times

Hauliers faced significant delays at UK ports as new post-Brexit border checks set in. With the UK having formally left the customs union, lorry drivers moving goods between the EU and UK were required to carry enhanced paperwork, including health certificates and access permits. John Simkins, general manager of Transmec UK, said, 'ultimately there's now an enormous layer of bureaucracy on both sides of the channel.'

Communities Secretary Robert Jenrick announced that the government was planning new laws to protect statues following the toppling of a monument to a slave trader during Black Lives Matter protests. 'What has stood for generations should be considered thoughtfully,' Jenrick wrote, 'not removed on a whim or at the behest of a baying mob.' In response, the government was accused of starting a culture war to distract from the pandemic. Historian David Olusoga tweeted, 'it's almost as if they want to distract people from their lethally failed response to the pandemic and the consequences of a disastrous Brexit.'

17 January 2021
Ben Jennings
Guardian

20 January 2021
Patrick Blower
Telegraph

Donald Trump departed the White House for the last time as president. As he left, Trump gave a speech highlighting his 'amazing achievements' and vowed that he 'would be back in some form', but also wished the Biden administration 'great luck and success'. Trump was the first president since 1869 not to attend his successor's inauguration. After leaving the White House, Trump flew to his Mar-a-Lago golf club in Palm Beach.

On 20 January, Joe Biden was inaugurated as the 46th President of the United States. Biden pledged to use his first 100 days in office to pursue a radical energy and climate change agenda. This included reversing many of Donald Trump's climate policies by re-joining the Paris Agreement, blocking a permit for a crude oil pipeline, and setting the US on a path to net-zero greenhouse emissions by 2050. In his augural address Biden said, 'A cry for survival comes from the planet itself.'

21 January 2021
Kevin Kallaugher
Economist

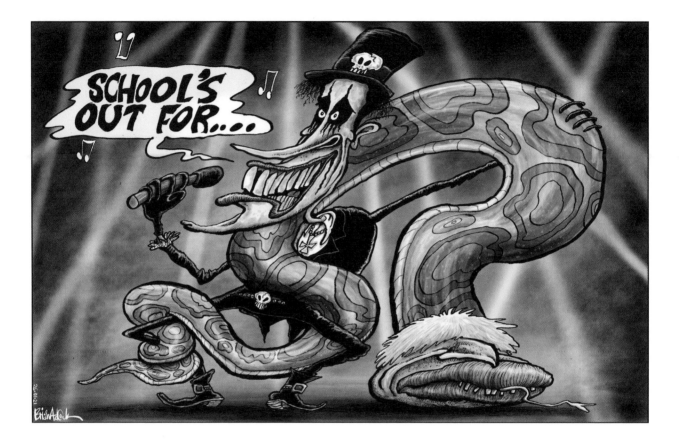

A Number 10 spokesperson announced that it was unlikely schools would be able to reopen until at least March. In response, children's advocates asked the government to set out a more specific plan to allow children back into schools. The children's commissioner, Anne Longfield, pointed out that lockdown was significantly widening the gap between disadvantaged pupils and their peers and causing a spike in mental health problems, with one in six children now experiencing issues. 'School's Out' was a 1972 hit for Alice Cooper who often performed with a snake around his neck.

26 January 2021
Brian Adcock
Independent

WHO DO YOU THINK YOU ARE KIDDING . . .

The EU warned it could restrict the export of vaccines after the bloc started to fall behind on its vaccination targets. Both AstraZeneca and Pfizer-BioNTech warned that they could not produce the volume of vaccines originally promised, prompting EU leaders to demand 'fair distribution'. The Oxford-AstraZeneca vaccine was mainly produced in the UK, while the UK's supplies of the Pfizer-BioNTech vaccine came from Belgium. The cartoon references the opening credits and lyrics of *Dad's Army,* a sitcom about the British Home Guard during the Second World War.

27 January 2021
Paul Thomas
Daily Mail

28 January 2021
Dave Brown
Independent

On 26 January, Boris Johnson confirmed that the UK's coronavirus death toll had now surpassed 100,000. The prime minister said that he was 'deeply sorry for every lost life', although there were some who questioned whether Johnson's apology was sincere or equivalent to crying crocodile tears. Labour leader Sir Keir Starmer said the figure was a 'national tragedy' and the Liberal Democrat leader Ed Davey called for an independent inquiry. The UK had the fifth highest number of deaths in the world at that time.

According to the cartoonist, 'Boris Johnson seemed to have belatedly realised, amid dreadful polling, that he and his "Conservative and Unionist" party were leading the UK into a future of independent states . . . The solution in his mind – obviously – a charm offensive. He trotted off to Scotland to look silly in some industrial work wear and do his wonder. However, First Minister Sturgeon wondered whether – in the middle of a Covid pandemic and lockdown – his trip was entirely necessary.'

29 January 2021
Andy Davey
Telegraph

30 January 2021
Kevin Kallaugher
Economist

More than 100,000 people took part in protests across Russia over the jailing of the opposition leader Alexei Navalny. Navalny had been arrested on his return to Russia from Berlin after recovering from a poisoning attack. The protests were the largest display of dissent in recent years and took place against a backdrop of declining freedoms and rising poverty levels. Over 3,700 people were detained by police as they tried to shut down unsanctioned rallies across 10 time zones.

Boris Johnson and the Conservative Party regained a lead in opinion polls following the early success of the vaccination programme. Labour had been hoping to poll ahead but the government's popularity grew by four points to 41 per cent – referred to by many as a 'vaccine bounce'. The latest data suggested the government's vaccination programme was gathering pace and on course to inoculate all over-50s by the spring. The coronavirus death toll, however, was still high, with 1,245 deaths recorded on 29 January.

1 February 2021
Ben Jennings
Guardian

Captain Sir Tom Moore passed away aged 100 after testing positive for coronavirus. The army veteran had won a place in the nation's heart after he set out to raise £1,000 for the NHS by walking 100 lengths of his garden during lockdown. He eventually raised over £32 million. The Queen led tributes to Moore recognising 'the inspiration he provided for the whole nation and others across the world.' Captain Tom will also be remembered for his mantra, 'Tomorrow will be a good day.'

3 February 2021
Peter Brookes
The Times

Polling suggested that the former Labour leader, Jeremy Corbyn, had been perceived during the last election as too unpatriotic, driving voters to the Conservative Party. A leaked Labour strategy document indicated that Sir Keir Starmer could turn the tide through greater 'use of the flag, veterans, dressing smartly at the war memorial etc'. 'I'm really proud of my country and I wouldn't be leader of the Labour Party if I wasn't patriotic,' Starmer commented.

4 February 2021
Patrick Blower
Telegraph

7 February 2021
Chris Riddell
Observer

Michael Gove warned that 'urgent action' was needed to resolve tensions caused by the Northern Ireland Protocol. Since the Brexit agreement, Northern Ireland had remained in the EU single market while the rest of the UK left, meaning checks were carried out on some goods entering Northern Ireland from Britain. According to Gove, this was causing 'serious problems'. He also warned that trust had been 'eroded' after the EU threatened to trigger an emergency provision in the Brexit agreement to control the export of coronavirus vaccines across the Irish border.

A group of Conservative MPs called for all coronavirus restrictions to be lifted by May 2021, by which time over-50s were expected to have been vaccinated. However, Professor Graham Medley, a member of the Scientific Advisory Group for Emergencies (SAGE), urged the government to 'make decisions dependent on the circumstances, rather than being driven by a calendar of wanting to do things'. Nearly 10.5 million people had received a first dose of the vaccine by 6 February. However, there were also around 1,000 deaths reported each day.

8 February 2021
Steve Bright
Sun

THE BEAST FROM SOUTH AFRICA...

8 February 2021
Christian Adams
Evening Standard

The first cases of the South African coronavirus variant were recorded in the UK, which scientists believed to be more infectious and more resistant to vaccines. Indeed, an early trial of the Oxford-AstraZeneca vaccine suggested that it offered only 'minimal protection' from the virus, but it did protect against severe disease. More than 100 cases of the South African variant were detected in the UK, leading many to suggest that an annual booster vaccine would be necessary to protect against variants.

New restrictions on travel came into force in order to limit the spread of coronavirus variants. Travellers entering the UK from red-listed countries were forced to quarantine in a hotel for ten days at a cost of £1,750. Holidaymakers caught flouting the rules faced fines of £10,000 or up to 10 years in prison. Jonathan Ashworth, the shadow health secretary, accused the government of not going far enough and urged them to '[secure] our borders to isolate new variants'.

10 February 2021
Patrick Blower
Telegraph

12 February 2021
Dave Brown
Independent

Matt Hancock announced plans for an extensive reorganisation of the NHS which would centralise power in the hands of government ministers. The health secretary argued that coronavirus had highlighted the need for a new approach to health and social care. However, the timing of the shake-up was criticised by Dr David Wrigley, vice-chair of the British Medical Association, who said 'It sort of beggars belief really, that this is happening at this time when the NHS is in turmoil.'

In Myanmar, the military seized power from the democratically elected leader Aung San Suu Kyi. Suu Kyi was detained along with other members of her National League for Democracy Party. In response, hundreds of thousands of Myanmar's citizens took to the streets to protest, but the military used water cannons, rubber bullets and live ammunition to restore control. UN Human Rights Council investigator Andrew Thomas warned that the people of Myanmar were in 'great peril'.

13 February 2021
Ingram Pinn
Financial Times

THE ELEPHANT IN THE ROOM

The US Senate voted to acquit Donald Trump in his impeachment trial, where he stood accused of inciting an insurrection at the Capitol. Many commentators said that the result confirmed the influence Trump still held over the Republican Party, with only seven Republicans voting to convict. One poll indicated that 69 per cent of Republican voters would be less likely to vote for any candidate who had found the former president guilty. Trump had become the first US president in history to be impeached twice.

15 February 2021
Nicola Jennings
Guardian

The Duke and Duchess of Sussex announced that they would be telling their story for the first time in an interview with Oprah Winfrey. It would be their first interview since stepping down as senior royals. They also announced that they were expecting their second child. In 2020 the couple signed a deal with Netflix reportedly worth up to $150 million to produce films and TV series. This came after Harry and Meghan vowed to become financially independent in their new lives away from the royal family.

20 February 2021
Ben Jennings
i

According to the cartoonist, 'Boris Johnson announced his "roadmap to freedom" but insisted that it would be determined by "data not dates" . . . Johnson would not know data if it kicked him in the pants (which it may yet do). Scientists laid his path to the sunlit uplands of freedom but it would be a miracle if he actually followed it. Little Matty Hancock struggles behind in his own incomprehensible way, a Boswell to Johnson's Johnson.' James Boswell documented his 83-day journey through the Hebrides with his friend and literary heavyweight Dr Samuel Johnson.

21 February 2021
Andy Davey
Telegraph

Sir Keir Starmer gave a speech highlighting the Labour Party's alternative plan for national recovery. However, many criticised the speech for being too modest and too easy on the government. Guardian columnist Tom Kibasi wrote that the 'Tories have been let off the hook for their disastrous mismanagement of the pandemic and for their dire Brexit deal.' The Labour leader had previously refused to criticise Boris Johnson's coronavirus plan because it was 'right that there's one communication that's coming out on a cross-party basis.'

21 February 2021
Chris Riddell
Observer

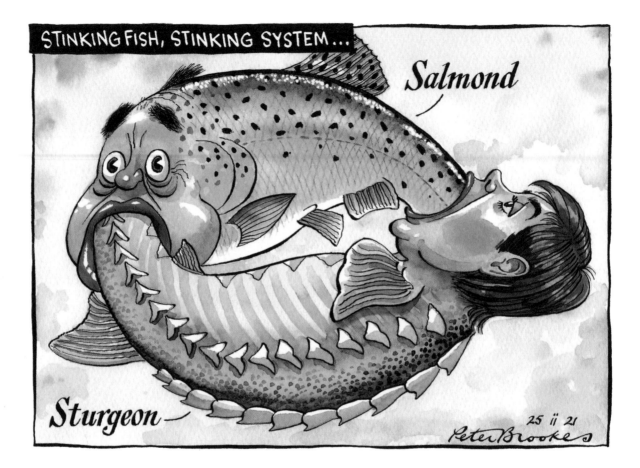

STINKING FISH, STINKING SYSTEM...

Salmond

Sturgeon

25 ii 21

Peter Brookes

25 February 2021
Peter Brookes
The Times

Scottish First Minister Nicola Sturgeon accused her predecessor, Alex Salmond, of peddling 'wild, untrue and baseless' claims that she was involved in a conspiracy against him. Both were due to give evidence at an inquiry over the handling of sexual harassment complaints against Salmond. The controversy broke out when the Crown Office urged officials to redact a piece of Salmond's evidence, a move that Salmond said proved the Crown Office was suppressing evidence to help the government. Opposition parties accused both the Scottish government and Salmond of avoiding scrutiny.

"THE END REALLY IS IN SIGHT"

Boris Johnson announced the government's 'cautious but irreversible' plan to lift coronavirus restrictions in England. From 8 March 2021 schools could reopen and two people from different households could meet outdoors. From 29 March outdoor gatherings of up to six people could take place. On 17 May two households could meet indoors and hospitality venues could reopen. It was hoped that all restrictions could be lifted from 21 June. The prime minister said that the plan was a 'one-way road to freedom'.

26 February 2021
Ingram Pinn
Financial Times

ROYAL WAFFLE MACHINE

Prince Harry was interviewed by talk show host James Corden on a double-decker bus tour of Los Angeles. The interview was aired after the announcement that the Duke and Duchess of Sussex would not be resuming royal duties. Harry revealed that he had taken the decision after the UK press created a 'toxic' environment that was 'destroying [his] mental health'. Harry also divulged that the Queen had gifted Archie a waffle-maker for Christmas. Since leaving the UK, the royal couple had set up their Archewell organisation for their non-profit work and new business interests.

27 February 2021
Paul Thomas
Daily Mail

In advance of his budget on 3 March, Chancellor Rishi Sunak warned that the coronavirus pandemic had taken an 'enormous toll' on the economy. Sunak pledged to 'level with the people' about the scale of the problem but he also vowed to continue to 'protect people, families and businesses'. The Office for Budget Responsibility estimated that annual government borrowing could reach £395 billion for the financial year ending in March – the highest since the Second World War.

1 March 2021
Brian Adcock
Independent

3 March 2021
Steve Bell
Guardian

Former French president, Nicolas Sarkozy, was sentenced to three years in prison after he was convicted of trying to bribe a judge. Prosecutors argued that Sarkozy had arranged a prestigious job for the judge in exchange for information about another case in which Sarkozy was accused of accepting illicit campaign donations. The former president remains free while his lawyers appeal the decision, a process that could take years. Sarkozy was also involved in a third trial, the so-called Bygmalion affair, where he stood accused of concealing massive overspending on his 2012 presidential campaign.

In the run up to the chancellor's budget it was revealed that the government planned to increase NHS salaries by just 1 per cent. The Royal College of Nursing said a pay rise 'as poor as this' would amount to only a £3.50 per week pay increase for an experienced nurse. Referring to the weekly 'clap for carers', London Mayor Sadiq Khan tweeted that, 'After all the clapping and all the praise, our NHS staff deserve more than this.' Boris Johnson said the government was giving 'as much as we can' in these 'tough times'.

6 March 2021
Ben Jennings
i

The Duke and Duchess of Sussex's interview with Oprah Winfrey aired on 7 March. During the interview they made potentially devastating claims about the monarchy. Harry and Meghan claimed that a member of the family had made racist remarks about their son and that Meghan had been denied help with her mental health. Harry also said that he was 'let down' by his father, Prince Charles, whom he claimed had cut him off financially and stopped taking his calls. Royal biographer Penny Junor said the couple had 'lobbed a hand grenade into the family'.

9 March 2021
Graeme Bandeira
Yorkshire Post

Unlocking too early could lead to a significant increase in coronavirus deaths, warned Professor Chris Whitty. The chief medical officer revealed that models showed that lifting restrictions too early would lead to a surge in infections among the unvaccinated, and even a gradual lifting of restrictions could lead to another 30,000 deaths before the summer of 2022. 'It is very easy to forget how quickly things can turn bad,' he warned. The Covid Recovery Group, which includes over 70 MPs, had been pushing the prime minister to relax restrictions more quickly.

10 March 2021
Patrick Blower
Telegraph

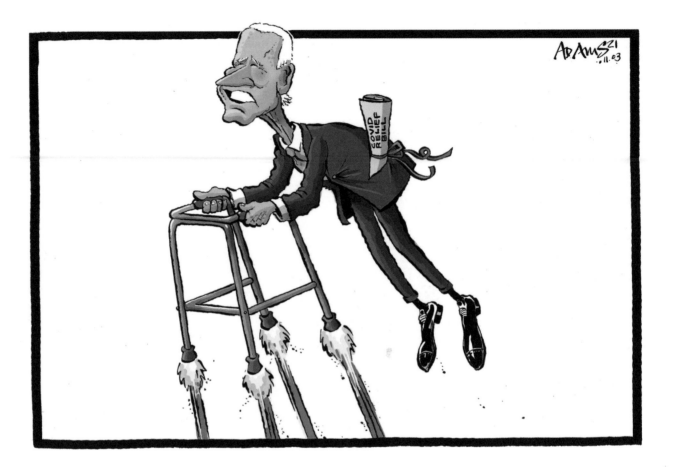

President Joe Biden's $1.9 trillion relief plan cleared its final hurdle in the US Congress. The House of Representatives voted to approve the massive economic aid plan which was designed to help Americans deal with the impact of coronavirus. Passage of the bill marked the first major legislative achievement of the new administration. Biden said that the bill would give 'the backbone of this nation – the essential workers, the working people who built this country . . . a fighting chance'.

11 March 2021
Christian Adams
Evening Standard

TEST & TRACE ...

The Public Accounts Committee protested that there was 'no clear evidence' that the Test and Trace scheme was having any impact on coronavirus transmissions, even though the government set aside £37 billion to pay for it. The committee said the spending was 'unimaginable' and pointed out that there had been two further lockdowns since the scheme was set up. Baroness Dido Harding, who ran NHS Test and Trace, responded that the scheme was 'an essential component in the fight against Covid' and that the large sums had been necessary to deliver testing on a large scale.

11 March 2021
Dave Brown
Independent

APOLOGIES TO ELIZABETH BUTLER — © Steve Bell 2021·12·3·4603·

ROYALTY - LEADING THE CHARGE AGAINST SNOBBERY, GREED AND RACISM SINCE 1066

- Belltoons.co.uk -

'We're very much not a racist family,' insisted Prince William following accusations made by the Duke and Duchess of Sussex. During their TV interview with Oprah Winfrey, Harry and Meghan claimed that a senior royal had expressed concerns over 'how dark' their son's skin might be. They also claimed that Archie was denied the title of prince because he was mixed-race. Buckingham Palace responded that 'recollections may vary'. The cartoon is inspired by Elizabeth Butler's painting, *Scotland Forever!*, depicting the charge of the Royal Scots Greys at the Battle of Waterloo in 1815.

12 March 2021
Steve Bell
Guardian

Piers Morgan left his role as co-host of *Good Morning Britain* after 41,000 people complained to the broadcasting regulator about his comments on the Duchess of Sussex. Meghan Markle alleged in her interview with Oprah that she had been repeatedly denied help from 'the firm' when her mental health deteriorated during her pregnancy. Morgan responded, 'I'm sorry, I don't believe a word she said.' Morgan was challenged on air by his colleague Alex Beresford, who alleged that Morgan was trashing the duchess after she severed social ties with him.

13 March 2021
Ben Jennings
i

Metropolitan Police Commissioner Cressida Dick came under pressure to resign amid outrage over police officers' actions at a vigil for Sarah Everard. Police broke up the vigil and grabbed and handcuffed some attendees as they held candles and phone lights aloft. Dick defended how officers had responded to the 'unlawful gathering' which posed 'a considerable risk to people's health'. Sarah Everard disappeared on 3 March while walking home in south London. A police officer was later charged with her murder. The incident sparked a public debate on violence against women.

15 March 2021
Steve Bright
Sun

HMS SPAFFWONGA

Boris Johnson announced that the government was lifting the cap on Trident nuclear warheads by 40 per cent. The increased limit, which takes the maximum number of warheads Britain can stockpile from 180 to 260, ended 30 years of gradual disarmament. The *Guardian* reported that the move paved the way for a £10 billion rearmament programme in response to threats from China and Russia. Trident missiles are deployed in four submarines, one of which is always at sea in order to respond to an unprovoked nuclear attack.

17 March 2021
Dave Brown
Independent

President of the European Commission, Ursula von der Leyen, was criticised over the EU's slow vaccine rollout. In response, von der Leyen threatened to withhold vaccine exports to the UK and criticised AstraZeneca for having 'underproduced and underdelivered'. According to the cartoonist, 'Ursula von der Leyen seemed to be every cartoonist's nightmare: good looking, intelligent, cultured, she embodied everything that Remainers were going to miss about Europe. But then she thankfully revealed herself also to be incompetent, petty, resentful and arrogant. We were back in business.'

21 March 2021
Peter Schrank
Sunday Times

Former Prime Minister David Cameron came under scrutiny after a report revealed that he had repeatedly texted the chancellor's private phone to secure special access to emergency coronavirus loans. Cameron was lobbying on behalf of financial group Greensill Capital, who reportedly paid Cameron over $1 million a year to act as an advisor. Most of the texts to Rishi Sunak's phone went unanswered. Greensill had also secured ten meetings with senior officials at the Treasury between March and June 2020 before ultimately filing for insolvency a year later.

22 March 2021
Morten Morland
The Times

As **CHURCHILL** NEVER SAID: "A **VILLA ABROAD** IS A **ONE-WAY ROAD TO FREEDOM**"

24 March 2021
Steve Bell
Guardian

A loophole in the coronavirus travel restrictions was dubbed 'the Stanley Johnson clause' after the prime minister's father travelled to his Greek villa to make it 'Covid proof' before the letting season. The latest travel restrictions included an exemption for people travelling abroad 'in connection with the purchase, sale, letting or rental of a residential property'. Labour MP Andrew Gwynne complained that it was a 'stick in the craw' for hardworking families that others can 'come and go if they have property abroad'.

In the US, two mass shooting events prompted calls to reform gun laws. Within two weeks ten people were killed during a shooting in Colorado, and another eight in Atlanta. In response President Joe Biden called for universal background checks and a ban on assault weapons. However, within hours some Republicans released campaign spots claiming Democrats were trying to take guns away from law-abiding citizens. The National Rifle Association is one of the most powerful political lobbies in the US, spending roughly $250 million per year, particularly on key Republican campaigns.

26 March 2021
Kevin Kallaugher
Economist

5,800 anonymous testimonials were posted on a website cataloguing acts of sexual harassment and assault in both private and public schools. 'Everyone's Invited' was set up to expose how children experience a 'normalised' culture of misogyny in the UK. Detective Superintendent Mel Laremore, Scotland Yard's lead on rape and sexual offences, said that the evidence showed that sexual abuse by pupils was a 'national issue'. The testimonials came to light following a week in which several high-profile fee-paying schools were accused of failing to deal with complaints about 'rape culture' in their institutions.

31 March 2021
Paul Thomas
Daily Mail

Sir Keir Starmer's first anniversary as Labour leader found his approval ratings at a new low. Polling found that just 32 per cent of voters were satisfied with Starmer's performance and the Conservative party now had a ten-point lead following the early success of the vaccination programme. Starmer's critics within the Labour Party claimed that he was too cautious, too bland and sat on the fence too often – perhaps, then, as useful as a chocolate teapot.

3 April 2021
Peter Brookes
The Times

The prime minister gave the go-ahead for a pilot scheme to test 'vaccine passports'. The system would allow people to access sporting fixtures, theatres and other public events if their passport showed that they had been vaccinated or had a recent negative test. Meanwhile, a review was launched into the actions of Somerset and Avon police after officers clashed with protestors at several so-called 'Kill the Bill' rallies. Demonstrators were protesting against a proposed bill which would hand greater powers to police, enabling them to shut down protests.

6 April 2021
Seamus Jennings
Independent

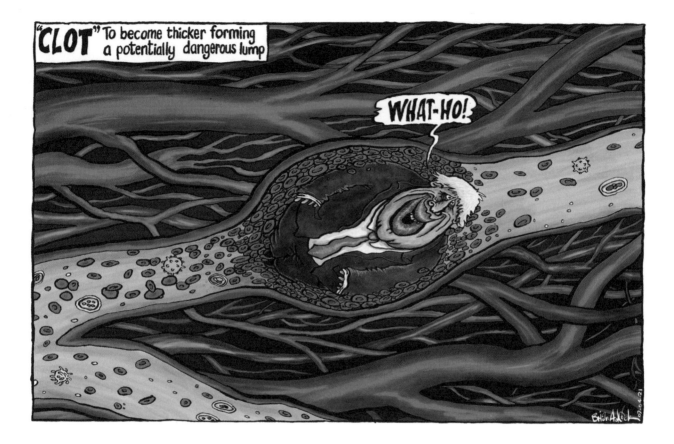

Britain's medicines watchdog said it had found 30 cases of rare blood clots in younger people who had received the Oxford-AstraZeneca vaccine. Those cases were found among the more than 18 million doses given. Fears over clots led the Netherlands, Germany, France and Canada to suspend use of the jab in under-60s. However, the World Health Organization reiterated that the benefits of taking the vaccine far outweighed any risks. Boris Johnson urged people to 'keep going out there, get your jab.'

7 April 2021
Brian Adcock
Independent

7 April 2021
Ben Jennings
Guardian

Families who lost loved ones to coronavirus established a vast memorial wall opposite the Houses of Parliament. The Covid memorial wall stretched for a third of a mile and contained around 150,000 hand-painted hearts, each one in memory of a life lost. In other news, new government guidance said that the Union Jack should be flown from all government buildings every day as a 'proud reminder of our history'. Critics said the Conservatives were more interested in symbolism than in fixing issues and were trying to deflect from the pandemic.

PROMISES, PROMISES...

No border in the Irish Sea
◆ Vote Leave

Brexit

Political leaders called for calm after several nights of violent riots in Belfast. 15 police officers were injured after being pelted with bricks, fireworks and petrol bombs, and a bus was hijacked and set on fire. Children as young as 13 and 14 were among those arrested. Tensions were sparked between loyalists and unionists over post-Brexit trading arrangements which created barriers between Northern Ireland and the rest of the UK. While lobbying to leave the EU, Boris Johnson campaigned alongside a 'Brexit bus' emblazoned with claims that the UK would be better off outside the EU.

9 April 2021
Peter Brookes
The Times

10 April 2021
Brian Adcock
Independent

Prince Philip, the Duke of Edinburgh, died on 9 April at the age of 99. The Duke was the longest serving royal consort in British history and he and the Queen had been married for 73 years. Prince Philip will be remembered for his dedication to public service but also for always speaking his mind. He once told an unfortunate photographer who was taking his time lining up the shot to 'Just take the fucking picture.'

'This is the return of Tory sleaze!' shouted Labour leader Sir Keir Starmer during Prime Minister's Questions. Starmer's outburst followed accusations that cabinet ministers had given David Cameron privileged access to lobby on behalf of Greensill Capital and that top civil servants were paid to moonlight for the financial lender. In the last year the government had been dogged by allegations of fast-tracking procurement contracts for their friends, rushing through planning applications for party donors and covering-up for ministers who broke the ministerial code. *Guardian* columnist Jonathan Freedland wrote that there was a 'pattern of corruption' at the heart of government.

18 April 2021
Chris Riddell
Observer

According to the cartoonist, 'The Church of England had been issuing NDAs [non-disclosure agreements] to cover up racist allegations and the government's race report turned out to be a shoddy white wash. Some indication of its shoddiness came from the number of experts cited in the report who were now rushing away from it . . . from leading public health expert Michael Marmot to Oxford psychiatry professor Kamaldeep Bhui, who damned the report as "really poor scholarship".' In March, a government-commissioned report was published which concluded that the UK 'no longer' had a system rigged against minorities. The United Nations called the report 'an attempt to normalise white supremacy'.

20 April 2021
Henny Beaumont
Guardian

12 major football clubs revealed that they had signed up to a breakaway European Super League. Arsenal, Chelsea, Liverpool, Manchester City, Manchester United and Tottenham Hotspur were among the teams involved. The move was widely seen as a power grab by some of the wealthiest clubs in Europe and was criticised for destroying the premise of open competition – the founding members would be guaranteed a place in the competition alongside just five qualifiers. Boris Johnson compared the league to a 'cartel' which was 'propelled by the billions of banks'. Meanwhile, campaigning was underway for local elections in May, with the Conservatives attempting to defend over 2,000 seats.

21 April 2021
Steve Bell
Guardian

21 April 2021
Christian Adams
Evening Standard

Leaked texts from Boris Johnson's phone were published in which he appeared to offer to 'fix' tax rules for the businessman James Dyson. Johnson suggested that Dyson employees would not have to pay extra tax if they came to the UK to make ventilators needed during the pandemic. He pledged, 'I will fix it tomo! [sic] We need you.' Johnson argued that he'd done everything necessary to secure ventilators and he had 'absolutely nothing to conceal'. In other news, Johnson scrapped plans to hold White House-style press conferences at Number 9 Downing Street, despite having spent £2.6 million on a new briefing room.

GOT HIS NUMBER ..?

Boris Johnson allegedly ignored pleas from officials to change his mobile phone number in order to prevent lobbying calls to his personal phone. *The Times* reported that Simon Case, the top civil servant, recommended the move a year previously amid concerns that it was too easy for MPs, lobbyists and business leaders to contact the prime minister directly. A source said that the 'extent of the contact was a consistent cause for concern.' Shadow minister Rachel Reeves called for an investigation into the 'special treatment' shown to those with access to the prime minister's personal number.

23 April 2021
Dave Brown
Independent

The Labour Party called for a formal investigation into how the prime minister had funded the refurbishment of his Downing Street flat. The prime minister receives an annual grant of £30,000 to spend on living quarters but there was speculation that Boris Johnson had spent up to £200,000 on the latest upgrade. Former chief advisor Dominic Cummings claimed that Johnson had planned to have Conservative donors 'secretly pay' for the work. In response, the prime minister insisted that he had covered the costs himself but refused to confirm whether the money had initially been loaned.

26 April 2021
Nicola Jennings
Guardian

The prime minister faced mounting pressure after several news outlets, citing multiple sources, reported that Boris Johnson had said he would rather see 'bodies pile high in their thousands' than have a third national lockdown. Defence Secretary Ben Wallace told ITV News, 'I don't give [the story] any credit at all.' Michael Gove also came out to defend the prime minister, saying he had 'never heard language of that kind'.

27 April 2021
Morten Morland
The Times

30 April 2021
Dave Brown
Independent

Arlene Foster announced she was stepping down as Northern Ireland first minister and leader of the Democratic Unionist Party. Foster had led the DUP's pro-Brexit campaign but had struggled to retain support in her party once the ramifications for the union became clear and the Irish Sea border came into effect. Foster had subsequently demanded that the Northern Ireland Protocol be scrapped but to no avail. The bowler hat and orange sash are symbols of the Orange Order, a staunchly unionist Protestant and political society.

Sir Keir Starmer paid a visit to the wallpaper department of John Lewis following a public row over the redecoration of the prime minister's Downing Street flat. *Tatler* magazine reported that Boris Johnson's then-fiancée, Carrie Symonds, had once called the flat a 'John Lewis furniture nightmare'. The couple had then reportedly spent up to £200,000 on refurbishments, carried out by interior designer Lulu Lytle. Starmer said that he was 'very proud to support John Lewis', but the Conservatives criticised the photo op as 'playing politics'.

30 April 2021
Christian Adams
Evening Standard

It was announced that from 4 May care home residents would once again be allowed to leave their homes for walks or garden visits without having to self-isolate for 14 days on their return. According to the cartoonist, 'This one came alive for me as an idea when I thought of substituting Steve McQueen's motorbike with a mobility scooter. I like quoting from films, but have actually never seen *The Great Escape*. It has since been pointed out to me that McQueen's daredevil stunt ends in failure. Perhaps this invalidates the cartoon, but I think it might add some poignancy.'

4 May 2021
Peter Schrank
The Times

Boris Johnson was all smiles when he arrived in Hartlepool before the by-election. Labour had held the seat since 1974 but their support had declined in recent years and polls suggested the Conservatives were now 17 points in the lead. While meeting locals, the prime minister spoke about the 'massive opportunities' brought about by Brexit, which was strongly backed by local people. *Mail on Sunday* commentator Dan Hodges wrote, 'One of the problems for Boris's opponents is they genuinely can't believe he's popular with people.'

4 May 2021
Christian Adams
Evening Standard

4 May 2021
Brian Adcock
Independent

The prime minister indicated that there would be 'some opening up' of foreign travel from 17 May, although the government was being cautious in order to avoid 'an influx of disease'. A new traffic light scheme due to be introduced would set the quarantine and testing rules for those entering England from abroad. However, a cross-party group of MPs urged the government to 'discourage all international leisure travel' as airport terminals could be 'a breeding ground for infection' and could lead to the import of new variants.

FLEXING MUSSELS AT BRUSSELS...

ENGLAND EXPECTS EVERY MAN TO KEEP HIS HANDS ON HIS OWN WINKLE!

Two Royal Navy patrol boats were dispatched to protect Jersey from a blockade by French fishing vessels in an escalating dispute over post-Brexit fishing rights. The 60 French boats blocked the port of St Helier in protest against new rules restricting their access to Jersey waters. In retaliation to the British response, France sent two vessels and also threatened to cut off Jersey's electricity supply. The *Independent*'s John Rentoul speculated that anti-French patriotism might serve the Conservatives well in the Hartlepool by-election, where legend has it that a shipwrecked monkey was once hanged as a French spy.

6 May 2021
Dave Brown
Independent

Labour suffered a shocking defeat in Hartlepool as the town elected a Conservative MP for the first time. Sir Keir Starmer was left facing questions over Labour's future, as early results showed that many lifelong Labour voters had also deserted the party in local elections. The elections were considered a test of the party's standing in key 'red wall' constituencies – those that had historically supported Labour. Labour MP Khalid Mahmood said it was a sign that the 'London-based bourgeoisie' in the Labour Party had 'lost touch with ordinary British people'.

9 May 2021
Chris Riddell
Observer

HUGGING

The Scottish National Party won a historic fourth consecutive victory in the Scottish parliamentary elections, but narrowly failed to secure a majority. The SNP vowed to push for another independence referendum, which Boris Johnson said would be 'irresponsible and reckless'. SNP leader Nicola Sturgeon replied that Johnson would have to 'go to court' to prevent it. ITV's Robert Peston reported that the prime minister's new plan to keep Scotland in the union was 'to love-bomb it'.

10 May 2021
Patrick Blower
Telegraph

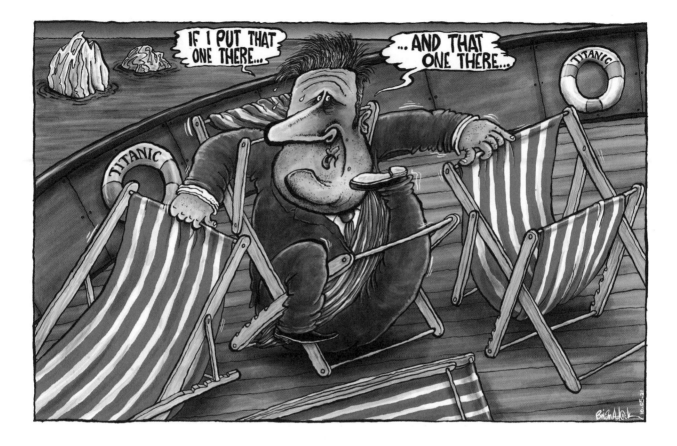

10 May 2021
Brian Adcock
Independent

Sir Keir Starmer reshuffled his shadow cabinet following Labour's disappointing results in the recent elections. The reshuffle was almost derailed by a reported power battle between Starmer and deputy leader Angela Rayner after it was leaked that she was to be sacked as party chair and national campaign coordinator. Rayner was eventually handed a major promotion to the role of shadow chancellor of the Duchy of Lancaster and shadow secretary for the future of work. The BBC's political editor Laura Kuenssberg described the reshuffle as 'a very messy affair'.

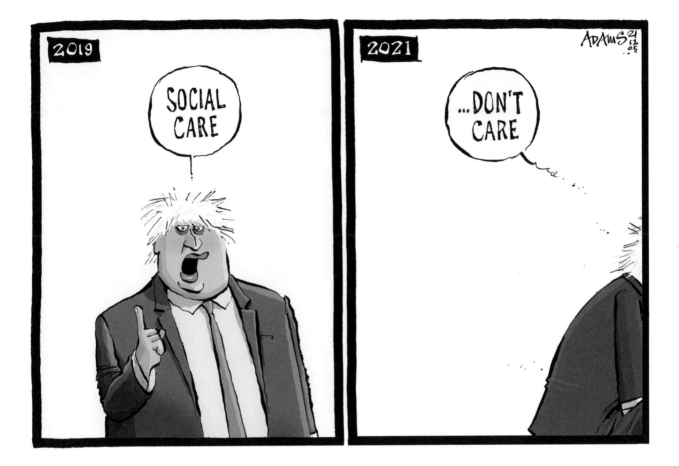

Industry leaders warned that care providers would either go bust or have to cut services after the government failed to set out plans in the Queen's Speech to fund social care. When he first became prime minister in 2019, Boris Johnson had pledged to 'fix the crisis in social care'. However, it was only mentioned once in the Queen's Speech 2021. Sir Keir Starmer said the lack of a plan for adult social care was 'unforgivable'. It came as official figures revealed that 21,677 care home residents had died of coronavirus during the second wave alone.

12 May 2021
Christian Adams
Evening Standard

The prime minister revealed that the public inquiry into the government's handling of the coronavirus pandemic would begin in spring 2022. Boris Johnson said that 'amid such tragedy the state has an obligation to examine its actions as rigorously and as candidly as possible' and 'learn every lesson for the future'. Co-founder of Covid-19 Bereaved Families for Justice, Jo Goodman, said the announcement was a 'huge relief' but that next year was 'simply too late to begin'. More than 127,000 people had died from coronavirus in the UK at this point.

13 May 2021
Patrick Blower
Telegraph

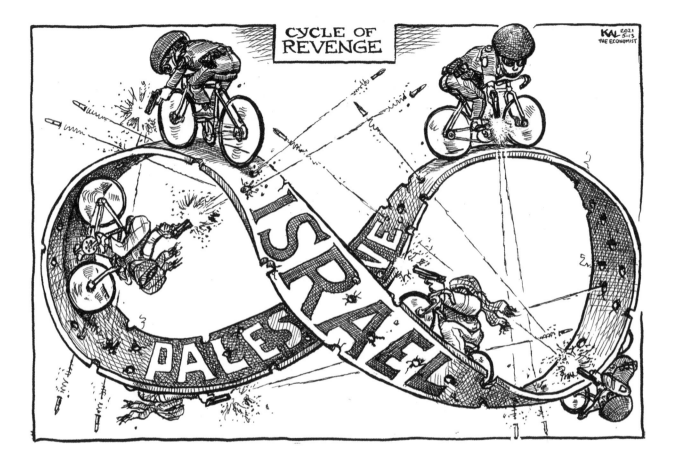

Following weeks of escalating violence in Jerusalem, Hamas, the Palestinian Islamist group that holds power inside Gaza, fired over 200 rockets towards Israel, targeting Jerusalem and other Israeli towns. Israel responded with dozens of airstrikes, including hits on residential buildings. More than 80 people, including at least 17 children, were killed in Palestine, with over 500 wounded. In Israel, seven people, including two children, were killed.

13 May 2021
Kevin Kallaugher
Economist

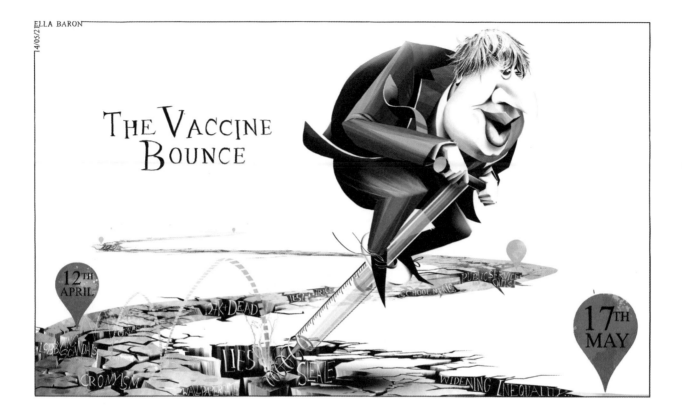

14 May 2021
Ella Baron
Jewish Chronicle

According to the cartoonist, 'As the UK approached step 2 of the roadmap to unlocking, the successful vaccination campaign that got us there also caused a surge in support for Boris Johnson. As a consequence, he led the Tories to a series of midterm election victories, including taking Hartlepool from Labour in a by-election. But the "vaccine bounce" in his approval ratings seemed to fly in the face of the appalling failures, inconsistencies and delays which characterise his government's earlier handling of the pandemic. As the credit for the vaccine extends far beyond Boris, it could be argued that he's merely ridden the wave of its success.'

17 May saw a significant easing of restrictions in England, but a new coronavirus variant was causing concern. Boris Johnson said he was 'anxious' about the Indian variant which had already been linked to 1,313 coronavirus cases. According to the cartoonist, 'This cartoon was published when many lockdown restrictions were being lifted. I did feel a bit like a party pooper. The question is: should cartoons be jolly and cheer us up, or should they be critical, point to the negative, be controversial? Perhaps in this case I went a bit too much against the prevailing mood of the day.'

17 May 2021
Peter Schrank
The Times

The Times reported that Sir Keir Starmer was considering starring in a fly-on-the wall-documentary to revive his standing in the polls. New polling indicated that just 17 per cent of voters thought Starmer was doing well. Andy Burnham signalled that he was ready to run for the leadership again and Diane Abbott called on the left-wing of the Labour Party to endorse him. Angela Rayner commented that it was time for a 'fundamental rethink'. Meanwhile, excitement was building for the much-anticipated *Friends* reunion, entitled 'The One Where We Get to See Our Favourites Back Together Again.'

19 May 2021
Peter Brookes
The Times

An independent investigation concluded that journalist Martin Bashir faked documents in order to persuade Princess Diana to agree to the 1995 interview in which she disclosed intimate details of her failed marriage to Prince Charles. It also lambasted the BBC for its 'woefully ineffective' investigation into Bashir's actions and for covering up his wrongdoing. The BBC and Bashir both apologised. Prince William responded that it brought him 'indescribable sadness' to know that the lies had contributed to his mother's 'fear, paranoia and isolation'.

22 May 2021
Morten Morland
The Times

Dominic Cummings repeated claims that the government was trying to cover up that it had pursued a 'disastrously misconceived' herd immunity strategy in the early days of the pandemic. The former chief aide also claimed that lockdowns may not have been necessary with the 'right preparations and competent people in charge'. Cummings was due to give evidence before MPs investigating the government's response to the pandemic the following week. He left his role in November 2020 after a reported power struggle at Number 10.

24 May 2021
Steve Bright
Sun

According to the cartoonist, 'After Cummings's extraordinary appearance at the Select Committee hearing, Johnson gave his full backing to Matt Hancock after the health secretary faced damaging accusations that he lied over the care home crisis at the start of the pandemic (and several other times). Johnson initially declined to respond directly when asked if Hancock was the right person for the role, but Downing Street later issued a statement expressing full confidence in him. It reminded me of those half-hearted endorsements of players by football managers before their exit. The "throwing under the bus" phrase was being used in the media.'

28 May 2021
Andy Davey
Evening Standard

Boris Johnson married his fiancée Carrie Symonds at Westminster Cathedral. Johnson became the first prime minister to get married in office for nearly 200 years. The wedding was said to be so secret that even close aides were surprised by the news. Just 30 guests were invited to the ceremony – the maximum number allowed under coronavirus restrictions.

Tennis star Naomi Osaka withdrew from the French Open following a row over her decision not to speak to the press. In her statement, Osaka revealed that she had experienced 'huge waves of anxiety' before speaking to the media. The organisers of all four Grand Slam tournaments had said that Osaka would be fined $15,000 for not attending press conferences and could face expulsion. Sir Keir Starmer appeared on Piers Morgan's *Life Stories* to speak about his life and career – a move that, according to *New Statesman's* Rachel Cooke, 'speaks both of his desperation and of a certain kind of ambition'.

2 June 2021
Peter Brookes
The Times

Education Secretary Gavin Williamson came under pressure after the education recovery commissioner resigned in protest over the £1.4 billion education recovery fund. Sir Kevan Collins had been appointed in February to oversee the catch-up programme for pupils who had lost out on learning during the pandemic. He warned that the government's support plan 'falls far short of what is needed' and the scale of the support was 'too small and will be delivered too slowly'. Daisy Cooper, the Liberal Democrats' education spokeswoman, said the 'pitiful' catch-up fund was 'an insult' and 'Our children deserve better than this useless education secretary.'

3 June 2021
Patrick Blower
Telegraph

The boss of the JD Wetherspoon pub chain was forced to deny that his business was facing a shortage of workers due to Brexit. Tim Martin had been a vocal Leave supporter but was quoted by the *Telegraph* as saying he now favoured a more 'liberal' visa scheme for EU workers to tackle staffing shortfalls – a comment which he said had been taken out of context. Many hospitality businesses were struggling to recruit as they reopened, a problem which, according to the trade group UK Hospitality, was exacerbated by workers from the EU returning to their home countries.

3 June 2021
Dave Brown
Independent

Boris Johnson faced a revolt as dozens of Conservative MPs backed an amendment to reverse cuts to foreign aid. The government announced last year that it was reducing the amount spent on international aid by £4 billion. This would mean that UK aid to Yemen, the world's most devastating humanitarian crisis, would be more than halved, funding for the Global Polio Eradication Initiative reduced from £100 million to £5 million and girls' education funding cut by 40 per cent on average. Meanwhile, the prime minister announced plans to build a national flagship yacht to promote British interests globally. It is reported to be costing £285 million.

4 June 2021
Peter Brookes
The Times

The prime minister was saved from a possible first defeat in the House of Commons after an amendment on foreign aid was rejected. Supporters of the amendment had argued that spending 0.7 per cent of GDP on foreign aid was established in law and part of the 2019 Conservative manifesto and so, in rejecting the amendment, the government risked breaking a promise as well as reducing the UK's diplomatic influence. Former cabinet ministers, senior backbenchers and all living former prime ministers were among those opposing the aid cut. David Davis MP said that, 'morally, this is a devastating thing.'

8 June 2021
Brian Adcock
Independent

Election officials announced plans for the biggest shake-up of parliamentary constituencies in decades. The aim was to bring every constituency's population closer to the average of 73,400 voters. However, opponents claimed that the plans would split long-established communities, with Sir Keir Starmer's constituency being one that could be significantly rejigged. One analysis calculated that, based on 2019 voting patterns, the changes would favour the Conservatives – leading some to accuse the government of gerrymandering. Ironically, the recent Conservative advances in the North and Midlands meant that the party could now lose out because of the changes.

9 June 2021
Dave Brown
Independent

President Joe Biden announced that 'the United States is back' as he arrived for the G7 Summit in Cornwall on the same day as a partial solar eclipse. Prior to their meeting, Boris Johnson promised that Britain would be 'a force for good' and a key ally to Biden. The day after Biden pledged that the United States would buy and donate 500 million doses, Johnson promised to donate vaccines 'to inoculate the world by the end of next year'. The two leaders also reaffirmed their commitment to the 'special relationship'.

11 June 2021
Ben Jennings
Guardian

Boris Johnson called for 'compromise on all sides' amid the continuing dispute with the EU over post-Brexit rules in Northern Ireland. The so-called 'sausage wars' now became a key part of the debate as, in line with the Brexit agreement, British-made sausages could now not be sold in Northern Ireland. According to the cartoonist, 'Sausages are basically funny. Journalists, and cartoonists in particular, love reducing complex issues to a snappy phrase or visual concept. So negotiations with the EU over cold meat imports into Northern Ireland became the "Sausage War".'

13 June 2021
Peter Schrank
Business Post

The government announced that it was delaying the final easing of coronavirus restrictions by four weeks to 19 July. Boris Johnson said that 'Now is the time to ease off the accelerator, because by being cautious now we have the chance in the next four weeks to save many thousands of lives by vaccinating millions more people.' It was also announced that second vaccine doses would be sped up. Meanwhile, the UEFA European Football Championship kicked off on 11 June, a year later than originally planned.

13 June 2021
Morten Morland
The Times

14 June 2021
Brian Adcock
Independent

Addressing the G7 summit, Sir David Attenborough warned that humans could be 'on the verge of destabilising the entire planet' and that G7 leaders face the 'most important decisions in human history'. Climate change had been one of the main themes of the summit, with the G7 group agreeing tough measures to phase out coal burning and to keep global temperature rises to 1.5 degrees Celsius. It did not, however, commit to sending the money to developing nations for climate assistance that had previously been promised.

UK FARMERS HUNG OUT TO DRY...

The government was accused of jeopardising the livelihoods of thousands of British farmers after it was revealed that a new post-Brexit trade deal with Australia would permit huge increases in meat imports before any protective tariffs came into force. Opponents also voiced concerns about a lack of detail on animal welfare and environmental safeguards. Emily Thornberry, the shadow international trade secretary, said the deal 'will send thousands of farmers to the wall'.

16 June 2021
Peter Brookes
The Times

President Joe Biden met for face-to-face talks with his Russian counterpart Vladimir Putin at what the two leaders agreed was a 'low point' in the relationship between their countries. Some controversial issues were raised in the four hours of talks, such as the recent cyber-attacks on American infrastructure, Russian aggression towards Ukraine and the imprisonment of Alexei Navalny. After the meeting, Biden said he thought there was a 'genuine prospect to significantly improve relations'. Putin said he had 'no illusions about the US' but he did see a 'glimpse of hope' for mutual trust.

16 June 2021
Christian Adams
Evening Standard

According to the cartoonist, 'Following the publication of Dominic Cummings's texts which appeared to show Boris Johnson calling Matt Hancock "fucking hopeless", the cartoon depicts Johnson and Hancock doing a *danse macabre* atop a field of Covid graves, as Cummings looks on, recording all on his phone.' The former chief aide published a new tranche of documents and texts that he said would combat the 'lies' from Number 10 about the handling of the pandemic. He also suggested that he would continue to campaign against the government's 'chronic dysfunction'.

18 June 2021
Rebecca Hendin
Guardian

John Bercow, the former MP and speaker of the House of Commons, launched a withering attack on the Conservative Party as he announced he was defecting to Labour. Bercow described the current Conservative Party as 'reactionary, populist, nationalistic and sometimes even xenophobic'. Meanwhile, the Conservatives suffered a shock defeat to the Liberal Democrats in the Chesham and Amersham by-election. The Conservative Party was accused of neglecting its southern heartlands – the so-called 'blue wall' – in favour of new northern seats. According to the cartoonist, 'I never had the chance to draw John Bercow when he was speaker. This is a shame, because he is a colourful and significant figure.'

21 June 2021
Peter Schrank
The Times

Matt Hancock resigned as health secretary after the *Sun* published pictures of him kissing a close aide in his ministerial office in breach of social distancing guidelines. In his resignation letter to the prime minister Hancock wrote, 'We owe it to people who have sacrificed so much in this pandemic to be honest when we have let them down.' Number 10 quickly announced that the former chancellor Sajid Javid would replace him. Javid said he was 'honoured' to have been selected for the post 'at this critical time'. After being cancelled in 2020, Wimbledon returned on 28 June, although the start was once again delayed by rain.

28 June 2021
Patrick Blower
Telegraph

30 June 2021
Ben Jennings
Guardian

Boris Johnson condemned the 'despicable harassment' of Professor Chris Whitty, England's chief medical officer, after a video was released of him being grabbed and intimidated by men in St James's Park while he struggled to get away. The home secretary, Priti Patel, said she was 'horrified' by the behaviour towards a 'remarkable public servant', while the vaccines minister, Nadhim Zahawi, said the 'thugs' should face charges. The Metropolitan Police were investigating the incident. Earlier in the month, Whitty was followed by an anti-vaccine activist who yelled at him for being a 'liar'.

Princes William and Harry were seen laughing and chatting together as they unveiled a statue of their mother, Princess Diana. The ceremony took place in the Sunken Garden at Kensington Palace on what would have been the princess's 60th birthday. William and Harry issued a statement saying, 'We remember her love, strength and character,' and 'Every day we wish she were still with us.' There had been reports of a rift between the brothers and Harry told Oprah Winfrey in March that the two were 'on different paths'.

3 July 2021
Steven Camley
Herald Scotland

The Labour Party won the Batley and Spen by-election by just 323 votes. Labour's Kim Leadbeater won the seat previously held by her sister Jo Cox, who was murdered in 2016. The result eased pressure on Sir Keir Starmer amid reports that there would be a leadership challenge from Angela Rayner if the party lost another northern seat. The Conservative Party co-chair, Amanda Milling, said that it had been a 'disappointing result' and confirmed that the Matt Hancock scandal may have played a part. 'It was something that came up on the doorstep,' Milling admitted.

3 July 2021
Peter Brookes
The Times

Boris Johnson faced criticism after posing for photographs with a giant St George's flag ahead of England's quarter-final game against Ukraine at the UEFA European Football Championships. Many took to social media to accuse the prime minister of hypocrisy after he failed to condemn fans who booed English footballers for taking the knee before games. Johnson said that those taking the knee in support of Black Lives Matter were indulging in 'gesture politics'. Others complained that Johnson had not shown any support for the Welsh or Scottish teams during the tournament.

5 July 2021
Ben Jennings
Guardian

On 8 July, Boris Johnson announced the end of Britain's military mission in Afghanistan after 20 years, even as the Taliban were rapidly regaining territory. Flag lowering ceremonies were conducted in secret as British personnel left. Johnson pointed out that the intervention had helped bring electricity, water and education to Afghanistan, with 8.2 million more children in school. However, he also admitted the future of Afghanistan was 'fraught with risks' as the Taliban advanced. The war in Afghanistan had claimed the lives of 457 British soldiers as well as 2,300 US troops and more than 50,000 Afghan civilians.

9 July 2021
Steven Camley
Herald Scotland

OWN GOAL...

DAVID SIMONDS

The UEFA European Football Championships came to a dramatic end on 11 July as England missed three penalties to hand victory to Italy. It was the first major final England had featured in since 1966. 60,000 fans packed into Wembley Stadium for the final despite social distancing restrictions. Boris Johnson defended the decision to allow bigger crowds, saying the game was hosted in a 'careful and controlled manner with testing of everybody who goes there'. However, a leading World Health Organization epidemiologist said it was 'devastating' to see the unmasked crowds crammed together.

12 July 2021
David Simonds
Independent

18 July 2021
Andy Davey
Sunday Telegraph

From 19 July, UK residents arriving from amber-listed countries no longer had to quarantine, with the exception of one country. According to the cartoonist, 'A loosening of quarantine rules was announced but this would not apply to France due to "persistent" cases of the Beta variant, so an "amber plus" category was created for a single country; France. I thought a handy cut-out-n-keep guide to Boris Johnson's increasingly baffling Covid-19 traffic light colours was necessary. I do my best to help.'

The government pressed ahead with plans to end all coronavirus restrictions on 19 July with a 'big bang' freedom day. But new coronavirus cases had soared to 50,000 per day. The NHS contact-tracing app had issued 530,126 alerts in the week to 7 July, a 46 per cent rise on the previous week, leading to a 'pingdemic'. The cartoon is based on Lewis Carroll's poem *The Walrus and the Carpenter*, in which the titular characters trick young oysters into following them along the seashore before eating them all.

18 July 2021
Chris Riddell
Observer

20 July 2021
Steve Bell
Guardian

Sir Keir Starmer backed a move by Labour's ruling National Executive Committee to disallow far-left campaign groups. Groups which promoted communism or claimed antisemitism within the party was exaggerated or demanded that the whip be restored to former leader Jeremy Corbyn were to be proscribed and anyone who remained publicly affiliated with them would be expelled. A party source said that the groups held 'poisonous' views, but critics claimed that Starmer was waging war on the left of the Labour Party which had strongly supported Corbyn.

Boris Johnson and Rishi Sunak were forced to perform a U-turn and self-isolate after coming into contact with the health secretary, who had coronavirus. Johnson and Sunak had initially said that they were part of a pilot scheme that allowed daily testing as an alternative to self-isolation. This caused an uproar among the public and opposition MPs. Many businesses said they may have to close due to the number of staff self-isolating after hundreds of thousands were pinged by the NHS app. Andrew Lloyd-Webber said that the theatre industry was 'on its knees' as two nights of his new show *Cinderella* were cancelled as cast and crew self-isolated.

20 July 2021
Christian Adams
Evening Standard

Nightclubs were allowed to reopen in England for the first time in 16 months. But, on the same day, Boris Johnson warned venues that, from September, anyone attending a nightclub or other large indoor event would be required to be fully vaccinated. Johnson said that 'nightclubs need to do the socially responsible thing', while Sir Patrick Vallance, chief scientific advisor, warned that nightclubs could be 'potential super spreading events'. 'So, "freedom day" for nightclubs lasted around 17 hours then,' commented Michael Kill, chief executive of the Night Time Industries Association.

20 July 2021
Morten Morland
The Times

In a BBC interview, Dominic Cummings claimed that Boris Johnson had fought against tightening coronavirus restrictions last autumn as 'the people who are dying are essentially all over 80'. The former senior advisor also alleged that Boris Johnson messaged aides that he no longer believed 'all this NHS overwhelmed stuff' and that he wanted to let coronavirus 'wash through the country'. Cummings continued his tirade against his former boss by accusing Johnson of putting his 'own political interests ahead of people's lives'. Cummings denied being motivated by revenge.

21 July 2021
Peter Brookes
The Times

FASTER, HIGHER, STRONGER - TOGETHER

25 July 2021
Morten Morland
The Times

A year later than planned, the 2020 Olympic Games opened in Tokyo – but the global pandemic continued to cast a shadow over the event. Before the games coronavirus cases in Tokyo hit a six-month high and the city entered a state of emergency. During the opening ceremony protestors carrying 'Lives Over Olympics' placards gathered outside Japan's National Stadium. Due to the rising number of cases, the games took place behind closed doors and athletes were asked to stick to strict social distancing guidelines. They were also required to leave Tokyo within 48 hours of their event finishing.

The 'pingdemic' continued to spread with almost 620,000 people being notified to self-isolate in the week to 14 July, the highest ever recorded. Test and Trace figures showed that over 250,000 people tested positive for coronavirus in the same week. The huge numbers of people self-isolating were causing staffing problems for businesses, and supermarkets struggled to keep shelves stocked. In response, the government had to publish a list of jobs exempt from self-isolation rules. Schools were also seriously affected – in the week to 14 July, 1 million children in England were away from school for coronavirus-related reasons.

26 July 2021
David Simonds
Independent

The prime minister unveiled new plans to crack down on crime and anti-social behaviour, proposing to have a named police officer responsible for every street, and to electronically tag thieves after leaving prison. Boris Johnson said he didn't see any reason why criminals 'shouldn't be out there in one of those fluorescent-jacketed chain gangs visibly paying your debt to society'. Two weeks earlier, Johnson had travelled to Coventry to deliver a speech on the government's levelling up programme. Coventry South MP, Zarah Sultana, described the speech as a 'meaningless soundbite'.

27 July 2021
Ben Jennings
Guardian

Thousands of anti-lockdown and anti-vaccine protesters gathered in central London for a so-called 'Worldwide rally for freedom' five days after lockdown restrictions ended. Conspiracy theorists David Icke and Piers Corbyn were among the speakers in Trafalgar Square. Former nurse Kate Shemirani made a speech comparing NHS workers to Nazis, saying, 'At the Nuremberg trials, the doctors and nurses stood trial and they hung.' Her comments provoked an investigation by the Metropolitan Police. Mayor of London Sadiq Khan called the speech 'utterly appalling'.

27 July 2021
Ian Knox
Belfast Telegraph

According to the cartoonist, 'The decision by Ben & Jerry's to stop selling its ice-cream products in the Israeli-occupied West Bank and East Jerusalem was met with fierce criticism from the Israeli political establishment, including a warning from the prime minister, Naftali Bennett, that the decision would have "serious consequences". Israel's foreign ministry called it "economic terrorism" . . . there is a long history of terrorism but now that dastardly duo, Ben & Jerry's, join their ranks. I thought the reaction was a bit over-the-top.'

30 July 2021
Andy Davey
Jewish Chronicle

According to the cartoonist, 'Severe flooding occurred in several towns, including London. The UK was already undergoing disruptive climate change with increased rainfall, sunshine and temperatures, said the Met Office (and anybody with sensory perception). The government said it would spend a record £5.2 billion on reducing flooding in England over the next six years, as the climate crisis increases the risk to homes and businesses. But what green policies does Boris Johnson actually have in mind? Will he tell us? . . . Meanwhile, he suffered an umbrella malfunction in fierce winds while at a memorial service.'

30 July 2021
Andy Davey
Telegraph

Gavin Williamson announced a £4 million scheme to extend Latin teaching in state schools to counter the subject's 'elitist' reputation. The education secretary said that learning Latin should not be 'reserved for the privileged few'. The government was also offering discounts on takeaways and taxi rides to encourage young people to get vaccinated. Michael Gove said that people who turned down the coronavirus vaccination were 'selfish' and putting 'lives at risk'. When asked whether he agreed, Boris Johnson said he did not, but that getting the vaccine was 'massively positive'.

1 August 2021
Ben Jennings
Guardian

Boris Johnson made a two-day visit to Scotland but did not accept an invitation to meet with First Minister Nicola Sturgeon – Sturgeon had only extended the invitation the day before Johnson's visit. According to the cartoonist, 'I like drawing Boris Johnson and Nicola Sturgeon, particularly together. They're such a contrast: Boris is dishevelled, shambolic and unprincipled; Nicola is immaculate, appears to be conscientious and competent, with perfect liberal credentials. Yet underneath, there is a sense of something darker: nationalism, a ruthless grip on power, some undemocratic instincts, perhaps. They could be more similar than we might think.'

5 August 2021
Peter Schrank
The Times

6 August 2021
Christian Adams
Evening Standard

Boris Johnson was widely criticised by MPs for joking that Margaret Thatcher had given the green energy industry a boost by closing coal mines in the 1980s. Whilst visiting an offshore wind farm in Scotland, Johnson said, 'Thanks to Margaret Thatcher . . . we had a big early start and we're now moving rapidly away from coal altogether.' Nicola Sturgeon said that the comment was 'crass and insensitive' as communities had been 'utterly devastated' by closures. The shadow foreign secretary, Lisa Nandy, called Johnson's comments 'shameful'.

Conservative MP Steve Baker, the self-proclaimed 'hard man of Brexit', declared that Brexit had become a 'fiasco'. Baker criticised the 'policymaking elite', even though he was Brexit minister from June 2017 to July 2018. Comedian Sue Perkins tweeted, 'Steve, I bring terrible news. It's your Brexit. It's your "fiasco".' Meanwhile, British musicians criticised the government for failing to reinstate visa-free work arrangements for musicians following Brexit. Sir Elton John said that, unless a solution could be found, the UK risked 'losing future generations of world-beating talent'.

6 August 2021
Dave Brown
Independent

ALL THAT GLITTERS IS NOT GOLD...

Boris Johnson praised Team GB's success at the Tokyo Olympics, saying it demonstrated 'there is no limit to what we can achieve', as well as Britain's 'sportsmanship, hard work and determination'. Team GB won 65 medals, two short of the record set in Rio de Janeiro, and achieved fourth place on the medal table. Meanwhile, Boris Johnson's personal approval ratings fell to their lowest level; a poll showed that 49 per cent of voters disapproved of the job he was doing as prime minister.

8 August 2021
Seamus Jennings
Sunday Times

Huge blazes forced thousands of people to flee their homes in Greece. Thick smoke could be seen pouring from the island of Evia, north-east of Athens, where acres of forest burned. 580 wildfires had broken out in Greece since July following a record-breaking heatwave. On 9 August, the UN had published a landmark study showing that human activity is changing the climate in unprecedented and irreversible ways. According to the cartoonist, 'Despite the deeply worrying subject, I enjoyed drawing this. I often enjoy drawing dark and pessimistic cartoons. It can be cathartic.'

9 August 2021
Peter Schrank
The Times

11 August 2021
Ben Jennings
Guardian

Prince Andrew travelled to Balmoral to stay with the Queen after being served with a lawsuit accusing him of sexually assaulting a teenage girl. Virginia Giuffre, an accuser of the convicted sex offender Jeffrey Epstein, claims that she was assaulted by Prince Andrew when she was underage and a 'sex-trafficking victim'. Giuffre's lawyers warned that the Duke 'cannot hide behind wealth and palace walls'. Prince Andrew stepped back from royal duties following the Epstein scandal in November 2019.

Boris Johnson allegedly threatened to demote Chancellor Rishi Sunak in response to a leaked letter from Sunak which contradicted Johnson's approach to travel restrictions. The report sparked a backlash among Sunak's allies who suggested that the Conservative Party could simply 'get rid' of Johnson following his poor performance in recent polls. In previous weeks, reports had indicated that the two men were at odds over how to pay for social care and execute the levelling-up agenda. When interviewed by ITV, Sunak declined three times to say whether he had leadership ambitions.

12 August 2021
Dave Brown
Independent

20 years since they were ousted by a US-led invasion, the Taliban began seizing territory in Afghanistan at an alarming rate, capturing ten provincial capitals in just a week. On 15 August, the Taliban reached the capital, Kabul, and President Ashraf Ghani fled the country. The advance prompted tens of thousands of Afghans to flee their homes. Those that left captured towns reported that the Taliban were killing men who had worked for the security forces and imposing strict rules on women. The cartoon references Joe Rosenthal's photograph of US Marines raising the American flag on Iwo Jima in 1945.

16 August 2021
Patrick Blower
Telegraph

There was chaos at Kabul airport, the main route out of Afghanistan, as people rushed onto runways to try to board flights leaving the country. The UK government announced a resettlement scheme to allow 20,000 Afghans to come to the UK over five years. However, Labour said the scheme 'does not meet the scale of the challenge' and risked 'leaving people in Afghanistan in deadly danger'. Home Secretary Priti Patel also hinted that Afghans who used 'irregular' routes to seek refuge in the UK would be treated the same as any other migrants.

19 August 2021
Seamus Jennings
Guardian

'YES, WE TRANSLATORS ARE IN A TIGHT SPOT NOW, CORPORAL – BUT THE IMPORTANT THING IS MR RAAB GOT THE HOLIDAY HE DESERVED'

20 August 2021
Paul Thomas
Daily Mail

Following the Taliban takeover, Western countries scrambled to evacuate their citizens as well as Afghans who had worked with coalition forces. However, the foreign secretary, Dominic Raab, was on holiday in Crete while Afghanistan fell to the Taliban. Raab insisted that he had been 'working tirelessly' during the crisis, but it emerged that he had delegated key calls about the evacuation of military translators to a junior minister. According to the *Sunday Times*, Raab had been ordered by Number 10 to return two days earlier but had stayed on holiday.

Sir Desmond Swayne was shouted down as 'a disgrace' in the House of Commons after he criticised refugees fleeing the Taliban in Afghanistan. Swayne asked Sir Keir Starmer if he would be 'queuing at the airport' if the UK were to be 'overthrown by a wicked and brutal regime', implying that Afghans should stay and resist. His comments were booed loudly. Tom Tugendhat MP, who served in Afghanistan, also spoke of the 'struggle through anger, grief and rage' felt by veterans as events unfolded. According to the cartoonist, 'I was secretly grateful to Desmond Swayne for saying such a crass thing in Parliament, as I was struggling for an idea before he opened his mouth.'

20 August 2021
David Squires
Guardian

Tony Blair, who had been prime minister when the UK joined the US-led coalition in Afghanistan, criticised the US withdrawal as 'tragic, dangerous and unnecessary' and said it would have 'every jihadist group around the world cheering'. Steve Bell's cartoon, depicting Blair, George Bush and Joe Biden, was not accepted by the *Guardian*. According to the cartoonist, 'I pointed out that I had already used this metaphor many times before' – as shown in the cartoon from June 2005.

24 August 2021
Steve Bell
Unpublished

A national shortage of lorry drivers caused major supply issues, with supermarkets and food chains struggling to get enough deliveries. Restaurant chain Nando's had to close some of its outlets due to a chicken shortage, which also caused Greggs to run low on chicken bakes. The Co-op's chief executive, Steve Murrells, said 'The shortages are at a worse level than at any time I have seen.' There was an estimated shortage of more than 100,000 lorry drivers, partly due to the pandemic but also because thousands of EU drivers left the UK after Brexit.

26 August 2021
Brian Adcock
Independent

ABANDONED...

Boris Johnson failed to convince US President Joe Biden to extend the deadline for evacuation flights from Afghanistan beyond 31 August. Several G7 leaders voiced concerns that thousands of vulnerable Afghans could be left behind because of the US timeline, but Biden commented, 'the sooner we finish the better'. Former defence minister Tobias Ellwood said the move should trigger 'soul-searching' over the UK's waning influence in Washington. Meanwhile, former Royal Marine Paul Farthing was successfully evacuated with 200 rescue dogs and cats, although his charity's Afghan staff were all left behind.

30 August 2021
Scott Clissold
Telegraph